Cloud Development and Deployment with CloudBees

Develop and deploy your Java application onto the Cloud using CloudBees

Nicolas De loof

BIRMINGHAM - MUMBAI

Cloud Development and Deployment with CloudBees

First published: December 2013

Production Reference: 1171213

Published by Packt Publishing Ltd.
Livery Place
35 Livery Street
Birmingham B3 2PB, UK.

ISBN 978-1-78328-163-3

www.packtpub.com

Cover Image by Romain Guy (romainguy@curious-creature.com)

Credits

Author
Nicolas De loof

Reviewers
Cyrille Le Clerc
Saeed Afzal
Rémi Goyard
Michael Neale
Mark Prichard
Harpeet
Spike
Aaron

Acquisition Editor
Joanne Fitzpatrick

Commissioning Editors
Poonam Jain
Nikhil Chinnari
Sharvari Tawde

Copy Editors
Alisha Aranha
Roshni Banerjee
Sarang Chari
Dipti Kapadia
Gladson Monteiro
Karuna Narayanan
Lavina Pereira

Technical Editors
Veena Pagare
Shali Sasidharan

Project Coordinator
Michelle Quadros

Proofreader
Ameesha Green

Indexer
Mehreen Deshmukh

Graphics
Yuvraj Mannari

Production Coordinator
Aparna Bhagat

Cover Work
Aparna Bhagat

About the Author

Nicolas De loof has been a Java Architect for 14 years in French IT Services companies. Being a techno-addict and an open source developer, he joined the Apache Maven team in 2007, focusing on the Google Web Toolkit plugin, and later the Jenkins community.

With many relations in the French Java community, he created BreizhJUG in 2008, which is a Java User Group in Rennes, France. Later, he founded the BreizhCamp, a two-day conference.

He joined CloudBees to contribute to an awesome project: running Java in the Cloud, from source code to production.

About the Reviewers

Cyrille Le Clerc is a senior software engineer at CloudBees with more than 12 years of experience in Java technologies. He came to CloudBees from Xebia, where he was CTO and Architect. He was an early adopter of the "You Build It, You Run It" model that he had put in place for a number of high volume websites. He naturally embraced the DevOps culture as well as Cloud computing which he implements for his customers. Cyrille is very active in the Java community, as the creator of the open source project embedded-jmxtrans, and as a speaker at various conferences.

Saeed Afzal, also known as Smac Afzal, is a young software engineer with more than six years of solid hands-on experience, specializing in solution architect and implementing scalable high performance applications.

He joined the IT field and started his career at a very early age. He is purely self-trained, and has moved forward with an entrepreneur spirit in different technologies in timely manners.

More detailed information about his skills and experience can be found at http://sirsmac.com. He can be contacted at sirsmac@gmail.com.

I would like to thank the Allah Almighty, my parents, my twin brother, and my life partner, Hafiza Zara Javed, for encouraging me.

Thank you to Packt Publishing for selecting me as one of the technical reviewers for this wonderful book. It is my honor to be a part of it.

Rémi Goyard started his career in 1998. Initially, he worked as a network technician (MCSE), then as a network consultant, he started his own Web agency (programming in PHP, HTML, JavaScript, and Hosting websites) in 2004. Today, he is a web architect at Sqli (Bordeaux), a French IT services company.

Rémi is passionate about Internet technologies, and keeps reading and learning to improve his skills. He likes teaching others (developers, marketers, project managers, and so on) to share his passion and help people to understand the Internet ecosystem better.

Being involved in the local developer communities such as Java User Groups, PHP User Groups, or JavaScript User Groups, Rémi likes to share his experiences, news, or business with others.

Rémi is also a blogger who writes about his tests and gives feedback on new web solutions.

Michael Neale has been developing software that goes in boxes and now to the Cloud for the past 20 years. He is a long-time contributor to various open source projects. He became a fan of PaaS Clouds from the minute he first heard about them.

In 2010, Michael along with others helped to start CloudBees. He didn't set out to build this, but only to use it! Since then, he has seen things grow in popularity as PaaS Clouds matured.

Prior to CloudBees, he worked at Red Hat on the Drools rule engine project and the Deltacloud API project.

www.PacktPub.com

Support files, eBooks, discount offers and more

You might want to visit www.PacktPub.com for support files and downloads related to your book.

Did you know that Packt offers eBook versions of every book published, with PDF and ePub files available? You can upgrade to the eBook version at www.PacktPub.com and as a print book customer, you are entitled to a discount on the eBook copy. Get in touch with us at service@packtpub.com for more details.

At www.PacktPub.com, you can also read a collection of free technical articles, sign up for a range of free newsletters and receive exclusive discounts and offers on Packt books and eBooks.

http://PacktLib.PacktPub.com

Do you need instant solutions to your IT questions? PacktLib is Packt's online digital book library. Here, you can access, read and search across Packt's entire library of books.

Why Subscribe?

- Fully searchable across every book published by Packt
- Copy and paste, print and bookmark content
- On demand and accessible via web browser

Free Access for Packt account holders

If you have an account with Packt at www.PacktPub.com, you can use this to access PacktLib today and view nine entirely free books. Simply use your login credentials for immediate access.

Table of Contents

Preface

All technology evangelists talk about revolutions. Even they just have a classic product to demonstrate. So, if I tell you that the Cloud will change the IT industry, you may consider that I'm biased, being a CloudBees employee. Anyway, I'm convinced that a huge shift has been introduced by the Cloud technologies and the way in which we develop a software and use it to host the application will enter a new age. To demonstrate my point of view, let's compare with another major revolution that changed the industry all around the world.

In the late 19th century, industry development discovered the flexibility of using electric engines compared to traditional steam ones. This was a huge improvement and was adopted for most of the activities. At this time, every manufactory has its own generator, sized to produce power for the engines they used internally.

2,170 Watts dynamo generator (Credit: Wikipedia)

With the adoption of electricity, sharing resources and concentrating on the generation of electricity was a natural shift from dedicated on-premise generators. This was a major improvement to reduce costs and to improve reliability and flexibility. First, power plants were created by large manufactories for their internal needs but quickly, a dedicated industry emerged, specializing in large-scale electricity generators.

From manufactories, electricity gradually began to be used for general purposes, and power plants became bigger and much more advanced to become the nuclear plants and giant hydroelectric generators we use today.

Three Gorges Dam hydroelectric power plant, China (Credit: Wikipedia)

Such a shift from on-premises generators has been possible thanks to specialization and standardization. Some incompatible standards still exist for power plugs and voltages, as some of you may have experienced while travelling around the world, but that's nothing compared to the early electric age.

In 1900, Paris was split into six regions, each of them with a distinct company to produce electricity for public lighting. Some of them used a direct current of 110 V, some others used a high voltage, as much as 3000 V. Some used two, three, or five wires to transport power to users. With power plants to concentrate into bigger companies, standardization helped to make electricity something that you don't actually have to worry about. If you don't have to travel to another continent—not considering myself traveling to London—you can use exactly the same electric device, without even thinking this could be an issue.

Nowadays, electricity is used as a service and you don't know from where it gets produced. You just rely on some standards to plug in your toaster and get it to work. You pay a bill per month, based on your actual use of electricity. You don't mind, when you buy a new washing machine, the amount of electricity it will require—maybe you should anyway—because you know your electricity producer will give you more when needed.

Automated computing is such a revolution and is getting even quicker. First, the computer replaced human beings for repetitive computational tasks. They were huge, complex, and dedicated mainframe machines. With large acceptance, some standards emerged, such as Unix/Posix compatible systems, and helped to reduce the dependency you had as a computer user on a specific hardware.

First, datacenters could be considered as equivalent to power plants; users didn't actually know where the computer was located physically and where they were connected to, on a vt100 terminal. They were just sharing resources, concentrating in a specialized location, with dedicated engineers and technicians.

Cloud is the next step. When Amazon creates a datacenter, it's about hundreds of thousands of computers that will be available for consumption using an API to rent them. You don't need to have a dedicated server anymore; you don't even have to estimate how large it has to be. You only rent one for your actual use and you can change your mind at any time.

The major shift with the traditional datacenter is that it's not just about grouping the resource in the same building, rather it's about sharing the resources for the whole world, without worrying about who is actually using them, and making it available using the 21st century power plugs, APIs—either de facto standard Amazon Web Services or open source OpenStack.

Cloud is such a big change that it completely changes our industry. There is no need to spend hours estimating our hardware requirements when a project is just a bunch of ideas that need to be prototyped. You'll have the adequate hardware available and can stop anything at anytime without any extra costs.

This book is a great opportunity for me to share my knowledge about the CloudBees platform on which I'm working as a support engineer. I'll guide you on how to discover the platform and show you its benefits for software projects, as well as the changes it allows you to make your development process more efficient.

What this book covers

Chapter 1, What's a PaaS and Why CloudBees?, introduces the concept of **Platform as a Service** (**PaaS**) and why this is the best place for a developer to start using Cloud services. We will also introduce CloudBees high-level vision of PaaS.

Chapter 2, Getting Started Quickly, covers setting up your CloudBees account and using ClickStart to get an application ready to develop within a minute. Also, it explores the services provided by the CloudBees platform.

Chapter 3, Users, Domains, and Services, explores the CloudBees platform from a user management point of view. It also covers the service ecosystem that makes the CloudBees platform extensible to match your requirements.

Chapter 4, ClickStart in Depth, gets deeper into the concepts of ClickStart and demonstrates how to use it in order to improve your own efficiency.

Chapter 5, Managing Your Build, demonstrates the use of the DEV@cloud platform to drive your project build and development workflow.

Chapter 6, Running Your Applications, explores the application-hosting service and options to manage your application scalability and security.

Chapter 7, Tools, demonstrates the advanced use of the CloudBees platform using the SDK, as well as other development tool integrations.

Chapter 8, Using ClickStack to Extend the Platform, gets deeper in to the RUN platform and its extensibility capabilities. It demonstrates how to select an alternate stack, customize, or create your own ClickStack.

Who this book is for

If you are a Java developer and want to explore the world of the Cloud, this book is ideal for you. This book will guide you through the process of developing and deploying an application on the Cloud. Prior knowledge of Java is essential.

Conventions

In this book, you will find a number of styles of text that distinguish between different kinds of information. Here are some examples of these styles, and an explanation of their meaning.

Code words in text are shown as follows: "The project skeleton is basically a Maven `pom.xml` file and comprises few classes."

A block of code is set as follows:

```
"build-with-jenkins": {
    "template": {
      "type": "https://raw.github.com/CloudBees-community/play2-
        clickstart/master/jenkins.xml"
    }
}
```

When we wish to draw your attention to a particular part of a code block, the relevant lines or items are set in bold:

```
"app-variables":{
  "proxyBuffering":false,
  "http_version":"1.1"
}
```

Any command-line input or output is written as follows:

```
git push heroku master
```

New terms and **important words** are shown in bold. Words that you see on the screen, in menus or dialog boxes, for example, appear in the text like this: "To create an account, www.cloudbees.com provides a **SIGN UP** link."

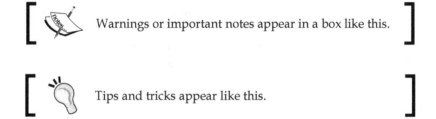

> Warnings or important notes appear in a box like this.

> Tips and tricks appear like this.

Reader feedback

Feedback from our readers is always welcome. Let us know what you think about this book—what you liked or may have disliked. Reader feedback is important for us to develop titles that you really get the most out of.

To send us general feedback, simply send an e-mail to feedback@packtpub.com, and mention the book title through the subject of your message.

If there is a topic that you have expertise in and you are interested in either writing or contributing to a book, see our author guide on www.packtpub.com/authors.

Customer support

Now that you are the proud owner of a Packt book, we have a number of things to help you to get the most from your purchase.

Errata

Although we have taken every care to ensure the accuracy of our content, mistakes do happen. If you find a mistake in one of our books—maybe a mistake in the text or the code—we would be grateful if you would report this to us. By doing so, you can save other readers from frustration and help us improve subsequent versions of this book. If you find any errata, please report them by visiting `http://www.packtpub.com/support`, selecting your book, clicking on the **errata submission form** link, and entering the details of your errata. Once your errata are verified, your submission will be accepted and the errata will be uploaded to our website, or added to any list of existing errata, under the Errata section of that title.

Piracy

Piracy of copyright material on the Internet is an ongoing problem across all media. At Packt, we take the protection of our copyright and licenses very seriously. If you come across any illegal copies of our works, in any form, on the Internet, please provide us with the location address or website name immediately so that we can pursue a remedy.

Please contact us at `copyright@packtpub.com` with a link to the suspected pirated material.

We appreciate your help in protecting our authors, and our ability to bring you valuable content.

Questions

You can contact us at `questions@packtpub.com` if you are having a problem with any aspect of the book, and we will do our best to address it.

1
What's a PaaS and Why CloudBees?

Cloud being the new buzzword, getting a correct definition is complex, and you can be lost trying to choose the best **Cloud** offers available on the Internet for [put your favorite stuff here]-vendors. Even talking about actual cloud implementations is difficult since there are multiple levels of them.

The concept of the Cloud is about the ability to get resources on demand without limits, but with the related cost, and without delays or human operation. Amazon Web Services is one of the most popular Cloud services, and with an adequate account set, anyone can get an **EC2 (Elastic Compute Cloud)** instance running to host applications or use an **S3 (Simple Storage Service)** bucket to store files.

Cloud services are commonly organized into three categories namely, **Infrastructure as a Service (IaaS)**, **Software as a Service (SaaS)**, and **Platform as a Service (PaaS)**.

Infrastructure as a Service

Amazon EC2 is a typical **IaaS**. This service lets users lean using simple API calls, servers to deploy applications, storage, or network routers. It only gives you the hardware, which you then have to manage to get your whole technical stack up and running. You have to select (or build) a virtual machine image (such as AMI) with your preferred operating system, configure network and routing, attach disks for persistent data, and so on. It looks like going to your favorite broker to buy PC components and build your own computer. The main benefit is that you only pay for what you actually use, so you can change your mind and get a bigger or smaller server, or just drop everything at anytime.

IaaS was a required, but low-level step in Cloud revolution. The flexibility it gives you is huge as compared to the bare-metal hardware, even with existing rent options. You can get dozens of servers available in few clicks, with ridiculous cost that only relates to the duration for which you actually use them.

The main drawback is that you only get the hardware. Operating system setup, low-level configuration, middleware installation, security, monitoring, and maintenance are your responsibilities. This makes sense if you have some very specialized software that you want to run, but for common technical stacks that are the concerned standards, this doesn't make much sense. If you need your own patched version of Linux kernel, IaaS is for you. If you want to run a Java application under the latest version of Tomcat, you will end up spending hours of engineering time just to set up and maintain the basic runtime that your developers are expecting.

Software as a Service

Another well-known actor in the Cloud ecosystem is **Google Mail**. Such software doesn't require installation; you access it with a standard browser using a secure HTTP transporter on the Internet. You can create a new Gmail address using a fully automated subscription process. Such services are called **Software as a Service (SaaS)** since they provide a fully running product, with some options to customize them, but are focused on a specific use case. You can customize Gmail's style for your company and set some default filters for all the users, but you can't convert Gmail into a CMS—it's a mailbox service, period.

SaaS is based on another standardization: web-based applications that run on modern, JavaScript-powered browsers. They can compare with the installed applications for user experience (at least, for those of us who don't run Internet Explorer), but don't suffer the same installation and maintenance overweight. SaaS users need not worry about installation of security fixes, backups, and maintenance.

If the project you're working on matches with SaaS offer, don't look any further; just use it. The time that you'll gain can be invested in lots of useful things to make your business successful. If your business is successful, and you really hit a technical limit, you will be able to switch to a custom solution, but don't try to implement your own general-purpose service if you don't have highly specialized requirements. Gmail users would never consider writing their own mailing system.

The drawback of SaaS is that you have limited options to customize the software. They all expose API so that you can programmatically interact with the service to integrate with the third-party tools and extend it to your own need, but you can't change the general service spirit.

Platform as a Service

Platform as a Service (PaaS) is a crossover between IaaS and SaaS. This is a fuzzy definition, but it defines well the existing actors in this industry well and possible confusions. A general presentation of PaaS uses a pyramid. Depending on what the graphics try to demonstrate, the pyramid can be drawn upside down, as shown in the following diagram:

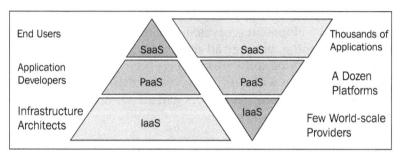

Cloud pyramids

The pyramid on the left-hand side shows XaaS platforms based on the target users' profiles. It demonstrates that IaaS is the basis for all Cloud services. It provides the required flexibility for PaaS to support applications that are exposed as SaaS to the end users. Some SaaS actually don't use a PaaS and directly rely on IaaS, but that doesn't really matter here.

The pyramid on the right-hand side represents the providers and the three levels suggests the number of providers in each category. IaaS only makes sense for highly concentrated, large-scale providers. PaaS can have more actors, probably focused on some ecosystem, but the need is to have a neutral and standard platform that is actually attractive for developers. SaaS is about all the possible applications running in Cloud. The top-level shape should then be far larger than what the graphic shows.

So, which platform?

With the previous definition of platform, you just have a faint idea; your understanding about PaaS is more than IaaS and less than SaaS. The missing definition is to know what the platform is about.

A platform is a standardization of the runtime for which a developer is waiting to do his/her job. This depends on the software ecosystem you're considering. For a Java EE developer, a platform means having at least a servlet container, managing DataSource to access the database, and having few comparable resources wrapped as standard Java EE APIs. A Play! framework developer will consider this as overweight and only ask for a JVM with web socket's support. A PHP developer will expect a Linux/Apache/MySQL/PHP (LAMP) stack, similar to the one he/she has been using for years, with a traditional server hosting service.

So, depending on the development ecosystem you're considering, platforms don't have the exact same meaning, but they all share a common principle. A platform is the common denominator for a software language ecosystem, where the application is all that a specific developer will write or choose on their own. Java EE developers will ask for a container, and Ruby developers will ask for an RVM environment. What they run on top is their own choice.

With this definition, you understand that a platform is about the standardization of runtime for a software ecosystem. Maybe some of you have patched OpenJDK to enable some magic features in the JVM (really?), but most of us just use the standard Oracle Java distribution. Such a standardization makes it possible to share resources and engineering skills on a large scale, to reduce cost, and provide a reliable runtime.

Cloud and clustering

Another consideration for a platform is **clustering**. Cloud is based on slicing resources into small virtual elements and letting the users select as many as they need. In most cases, this requires the application to support a clustering mode, as using more resources will require you to scale out on multiple hosts.

Clustering has never been a trivial thing, and many developers aren't familiar with the related constraints. The platform can help them by providing specialized services to distribute the load around the cluster's nodes. Some PaaS such as CloudBees or Google App Engine provide such features, while some don't. This is the major difference between PaaS offers. Some are IaaS-like preinstalled middleware services, while some offer a highly integrated platform.

A typical issue faced is that of state management. Java EE developers rely on `HttpSession` to store user's data and retrieve them on subsequent interaction. Modern frameworks tend to be stateless, but the state needs to be managed anyway. PaaS has to provide options to developers, so that they can choose the best strategy to match their own business requirements. This is a typical clustering issue that is well addressed by PaaS because the technical solutions (sticky session, session replication, distributed storage engines, and so on) have been implemented once with all the required skills to do it right, and can be used by all platform users.

Thanks to a PaaS, you don't need to be a clustering guru. This doesn't mean that it will magically let your legacy application scale out, but it gives you adequate tools to design the application for scalability.

Private versus public Clouds

Many companies are interested in Cloud, thanks to the press for publishing all product announcements as the new revolution, and would like to benefit from them but as a private resource.

If you go back to the comparison in the *Preface* with an electricity production, this may make sense if you're well established. Amazon or Google should have private power plants to supply giant data centers can make sense—anyway it doesn't seems that they do but as backends. For most of companies, this would be a surprising company choice.

The main reason is that the principle of the Cloud relies on the last letter of XaaS (**S**) that stands for **Service**. You can install an OpenStack or VMware farm on your data center, but then you won't have an IaaS. You will have some virtualization and flexibility that probably is far better than traditional dedicated hardware, but you miss the major change. You still will have to hire operators to administer the servers and software stack. You will even have a more complex software stack (search for an OpenStack administrator and you'll understand). Using Cloud makes sense because there are thousands of users all around the world sharing the same lower-level resources, and a centralized, highly specialized team to manage them all.

Building your own, private PaaS is yet another challenge. This is not a simple middleware stack. This is not about providing virtual machine images with a preinstalled Tomcat server. What about maintenance, application scalability, deployment APIs, clustering, backup, data replication, high availability, monitoring, and support?

Support is a major added value of cloud services—I'm not just saying this because I'm a support engineer—but because when something fails, you need someone to help. You can't just wait with the promise for a patch provided by the community. The guy who's running your application needs to have significant knowledge of the platform. That's one reason that CloudBees is focusing on Java first, as this is the ecosystem and environment we know best (even we have some Erlang and Ruby engineers whose preferred game is to troll on this displeasing language).

With a private Cloud, you probably can have level-one support with an internal support team, but you can't handle all the issues. As for resource concentration, working in support with thousands of customers allows a public platform to build an impressive knowledge base.

All those topics are ignored in most cases as people only focus on the `app:deploy` automation, as opposed to the old-style deployments to dedicated hardware. If this is what you're looking for, you should know that Maven was able to do this for years on all the Java EE containers using cargo. You can check the same at `http://cargo.codehaus.org`. Cloud isn't just about abstracting the runtime behind an API; it's about changing the way in which developers manage and access runtime so that it becomes a service they can consume without any need to worry about what's happening behind the scene.

Security

The reason that companies claim to prefer a private cloud solution is **security**.

Amazon datacenters are far more secure than any private datacenter, due to both strong security policy and anonymous user data. Security is not about exploiting encryption algorithms, like in Hollywood movies, but about social attacks that are far more fragile. Few companies take care of administrative, financial, familial, or personal safety.

Thanks to the combination of VPN, HTTPS, fixed IPs, and firewall filters, you can safely deploy an application on Amazon Cloud as an extension to your own network, to access data from your legacy Oracle or SAP mainframe hosted in your datacenter. As a mobile application demonstrates, your data is already going out from your private network. There's no concrete reason why your backend application can't be hosted outside your walls.

CloudBees – embrace the development stack

CloudBees PaaS has something special in its DNA that you won't find in other PaaS; focusing on the Java ecosystem first, even with polyglot support, CloudBees understands well the Java ecosystem's complexity and its underlying practices.

Heroku was one of the first successful PaaS, focusing on Ruby runtime. Deployment of a Ruby application is just about sending source code to the platform using the following command:

```
git push heroku master
```

Ruby is a pleasant ecosystem because there are no such long debates on building and provisioning tools that we know of, unlike in JavaWorld, GemFile, and Rake, period.

In the Java ecosystem, there is a need to generate, compile the source code, and then sometime post the process classes, hence a large set of build tools are required. There's also a need to provision runtime with dozens of dependencies, so a set of dependency management tools, inter-project relations, and so on are required. With Agile development practices, automated testing has introduced a huge set of test frameworks that developers want to integrate into the deployment process.

The Java platform is not just about hosting a JVM or a servlet container, it's about managing Ant, Maven, SBT, or Gradle builds, as well as Grails-, Play-, Clojure-, and Scala-specific tooling. It's about hosting dependency repositories. It's about handling complex build processes to include multiple levels of testing and code analysis.

The CloudBees platform has two major components:

- **RUN@cloud** is a PaaS, as described earlier, to host applications and provide high-level runtime services
- **DEV@cloud** is a continuous integration and deployment SaaS based on Jenkins

Jenkins is not the subject of this book, but it is the de facto standard for but not limited to continuous integration in the Java ecosystem. With a large set of plugins, it can be extended to support a large set of tools, processes, and views about your project.

The CloudBees team includes major Jenkins committers (including `myself #selfpromotion`), and so it has a deep knowledge on Jenkins ecosystem and is best placed to offer it as a Cloud service. We also can help you to diagnose your project workflow by applying the best continuous integration and deployment practices. This also helps you to get more efficient and focused results on your actual business development.

The following screenshot displays the continuous Cloud delivery concept in CloudBees:

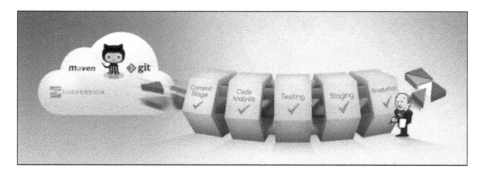

With some CloudBees-specific plugins to help, DEV@cloud Jenkins creates a smooth code-build-deploy pipeline, comparable to Heroku's Git push, but with full control over the intermediary process to convert your source code to a runnable application. This is such a significant component to build a full stack for Java developers that CloudBees is the official provider for the continuous integration service for Google App Engine (`http://googleappengine.blogspot.`
`fr/2012/10/jenkins-meet-google-app-engine.html`), Cloud Foundry (`http://blog.cloudfoundry.com/2013/02/28/continuous-integration-to-`
`cloud-foundry-com-using-jenkins-in-the-cloud/`), and Amazon Beanstalk (to be announced as I'm writing this chapter).

Summary

This chapter introduced Cloud principles and benefits and compared CloudBees to its competitors.

We will cover the CloudBees platform in detail in the next chapters. Hope that you will like it as we do and give it a try. If you prefer another PaaS, never mind; experiment with Cloud and let competitors give you the best service they can.

2
Getting Started Quickly

To avail all services, you need to set up a CloudBees account. This process requires some registration steps and an initial setup before you are ready to do something productive. This chapter demonstrates how the CloudBees platform has been designed to lower this barrier and bring you to active application development as soon as possible.

To create an account, `www.cloudbees.com` provides a **SIGN UP** link. Registration is a simple process as the base services are free, so you only have to provide a valid e-mail address and some personal information.

A user on a CloudBees platform is identified by their e-mail address. Once you sign in, you create a user and domain to host your resources. This domain is sometimes called **account** in documentation, but is not tied to the user, because the user can access multiple domains, and a domain can be shared between a set of users with distinct roles. When you select a domain/account name, note that it will be used in all your service URLs and is immutable. So choose an appropriate name—for example, your company or project name.

The following screenshot shows the account creation form:

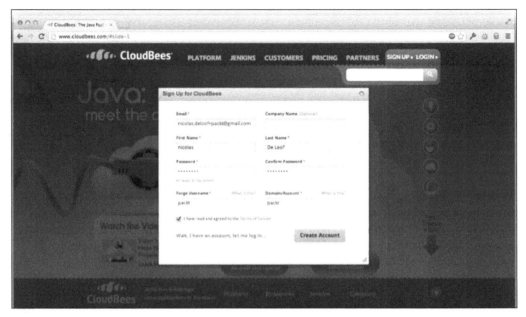

Account creation form

The domain creation form also asks you to enter a name in the **Forge Username** field. This username will be used to access forge services for HTTP-based resources (webdev, subversion, and so on). Read the terms of service carefully (as you always do in such circumstances, don't you?) and validate the form.

You are then redirected to `http://grandcentral.cloudbees.com`, where all CloudBees services and users cross, just like trains and travelers do at New York station. This probably could have been named `services.cloudbees.com` or something similar, but you know how engineers are.

The following picture displays New York's Grand Central Terminal:

New York Grand Central Terminal, credit: Wikipedia

Your CloudBees account is now successfully created. But you can't do much on the platform because the account is distributed among dedicated services that you need to enable. So, let's start getting some actual services from the platform.

Subscribing to services

The GrandCentral services menu lets you manage your subscriptions. You can add new services to your domain or change the subscription plan. For this quick setup guide, we will subscribe to the DEV@cloud and RUN@cloud services. The former covers the forge repositories and a Jenkins instance to manage your project build, deployment, and continuous integration, and the latter hosts our applications.

Provisioning these services, especially getting Jenkins up and running, can take few minutes, so let's explore the GrandCentral UI in the meantime.

Keys and authorizations

As part of user settings (a small gear icon at the top right of the window), an API key and a secret key have been generated for you as a CloudBees user. You will need them to use the SDK. We will discuss this in *Chapter 7, Tools*.

User settings also allow you to register your SSH public keys. We will use these keys to access Git repositories hosted on the CloudBees forge later in this chapter. If you don't have one, don't know what it is, and don't want to spend time on this, never mind; just jump to the next section and use HTTPS.

If you don't have an SSH key yet, you can generate one using `ssh-keygen` on Linux and Mac OS X or by using PuTTY on Windows. Be careful, CloudBees requires a key in OpenSSH format, so export your keys in an appropriate format. While using PuTTY on Windows, you need to use the export menu, as shown in the following screenshot:

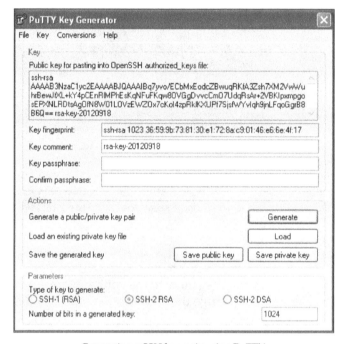

Generating a SSH key pair using PuTTY

Save the generated private key (by navigating to **Conversions | Export** in PuTTY, you should get the OpenSSH key) under `$HOME/.ssh/id_rsa`; Windows users will hit the stupid Explorer restriction that doesn't let them create a `.ssh` directory, even this is fully supported by the operating system. Sorry guys, you will have to run the `cmd.exe` console to create this one using the `mkdir` command.

Paste the public key pair on the CloudBees web UI. Windows PuTTY users will copy and paste it from the key generator text area. This key will be validated to ensure whether the format is correct.

 As we talk about the SSH key and authentication, you will see that such a key has also been generated for your account. We will use it from the DEV@cloud Jenkins to authorize the build service to access your own resources.

Accessing services

After subscribing to few services, if you let your mouse pointer hover over the **Services** menu without clicking on it, a pop up will show you all active services with links to access them. You'll use these links to navigate through the CloudBees services. The format for these URLs is `https://grandcentral.cloudbees.com/services/goto/<service>`, as GrandCentral will act as an SSO service to integrate both CloudBees and third-party services for a smooth user experience.

Let's check whether Jenkins is ready to handle our project by accessing the Jenkins link at `https://grandcentral.cloudbees.com/services/goto/dev-at-cloud`. The Jenkins instance is configured but has no job defined, so let's create a project now.

Hey, we already are in the middle of this **QuickStart** section, so it's time to accelerate and get some actual application running, don't you think so? We could spend some time here explaining how to create a code repository, set up a Jenkins job, and deploy our application, but let's get started and use a wizard-style automation to set up a new application—**CloudBees ClickStart**.

Setting up an application using ClickStart

On the GrandCentral welcome page, you probably noticed the big black **ClickStart** button.

This option gives you a list of available wizards to create typical applications based on a set of popular frameworks. From the list of available **ClickStart** options, you will notice that CloudBees is not just Java-specific, but we will discuss this further in later chapters.

So let's choose a classic Tomcat 7 **ClickStart** option for this guide as shown in the following screenshot:

ClickStart to get application set up in few clicks

ClickStart asks you for the application name and handles all the resource initializations to prepare a development pipeline for the requested framework. This means the following:

- Git repository, hosted on CloudBees forge, with initial code source is committed
- Jenkins build to compile, test, and package the application
- Jenkins deployer is configured to deploy the resulting artifact on RUN@cloud up on build success
- The RUN@cloud application is set with the appropriate runtime configuration and container type
- Database is bound to the application

The **ClickStart** wizard gives you status links to the generated resources so that you can explore all of them.

ClickStart status screen

Depending on the **ClickStart** option you select, the Jenkins build may use distinct plugins, build tools, and configuration options. Some **ClickStart** options don't use a database or do not rely on other services, but the general idea is always the same: set up the application as a continuous deployment pipeline, from source code to hosted application, with an initial working state. When the **ClickStart** operation is complete, an initial Jenkins build is run to confirm whether the pipeline is ready to support your own developments.

As we explained in the previous chapter, the CloudBees vision of a PaaS is about hosting the full development cycle, not just application hosting. With **ClickStart**, you can be ready to develop your own application from a validated skeleton in just a few minutes.

After **ClickStart** has successfully generated and configured all resources, you can see the app running on your RUN@cloud subdomain at `http://<app>.<account>.cloudbees.net`.

Getting the code

Let's now edit the generated **ClickStart** application to customize it according to our needs. The first thing to do is to get the source code to amend it with our own stuff.

We assume you have a Git client installed on your computer or use an appropriate IDE integration.

 ClickStart always uses Git for repositories. The CloudBees forge also supports subversion, and maybe you prefer another SCM, such as Mercurial. There is no enforcement to use Git, and you can switch to your favorite SCM just by changing the Jenkins job SCM configuration. CloudBees just doesn't provide this option in **ClickStart**. If you don't want to use Git, you'll need to export the skeleton project and commit code into your own repository.

The **ClickStart** wizard gives us the forge repository URL. Pick it up and use it to clone your project. To use SSH, you need to have a key generated and registered on the CloudBees user settings page as discussed earlier. If you don't have one, you can use HTTPS with your CloudBees forge credentials; but beware that your login is your forge login credential and not your e-mail address.

```
git clone <repository URL>
```

Making changes and updating the application

Let's edit the application sources and add our own stuff to customize it to our needs. On a basic Tomcat web application, *customization* is not the adequate term as the code skeleton doesn't provide much, and we have to configure our favorite web framework and utility classes; but at least, we have a base project structure to get started quickly. If you're familiar with **Maven archetype**, this is mostly comparable at this stage.

After making some changes to our app, let's commit and push it to CloudBees:

```
git.add
git commit -m "I made some changes"
git push origin master
```

 If you are not familiar with a distributed SCM such as Git, you just need to know that sending changes to a CloudBees-hosted repository is a two-step process:

* Commit the repository to group file changes into an atomic commit object
* Push it to send pending local commits to the remote repository

Now, let's have a look at our DEV@cloudJenkins instance. You'll notice that the build queue has immediately triggered a build, just as the forge received our commit. Such a post-commit hook allows Jenkins to be very efficient for continuous integration and build automation, since there is absolutely no delay in waiting after a commit is pushed and a build is run to validate it. Jenkins can also poll SCM, but for whatever repository you use, whether it's being hosted on the CloudBees platform or not, please consider using a commit hook for efficiency.

The build runs to integrate our commit, and the Jenkins deployer plugin deploys the resulting application onto RUN@cloud. We can check whether the application has been updated just few seconds after we've committed it, without any complex configuration to set up this process. We will discuss in *Chapter 5*, *Managing Your Build*, how to review this **continuous deployment** process to adapt to developer teams, multiple environments, and release processes.

PaaS versus self-managed infrastructure

Something you probably noticed during the introduction to the CloudBees platform is that you never interacted with a human to get resources provisioned or tools setup. Everything is automated and managed by APIs, therefore, full-platform automation, such as **ClickStart**, is possible.

Creating new resources on demand, like we did by creating an application and database on RUN@cloud, is possible — thanks to Cloud elasticity — and relies on the mostly unlimited resources that IaaS has to offer.

As compared to self-managed infrastructure built on an IaaS, the main benefit of a PaaS is the time you save by not handling low-level stuff. Your engineering team probably could set up a Tomcat server on an EC2 instance as well as a Git server on a Jenkins instance. They even can have this scripted some way, so this can be quickly set up.

But this is only the emerged part of the PaaS iceberg, and does not even considering the time spent to set up such an infrastructure. This won't include time and money invested in monitoring, maintenance, backups, upgrades, and support for the whole platform. They aren't as visible as the application you just deployed so are easily ignored when trying to compare with another solution. If you include all those topics in your self-managed infrastructure costs, it probably will be unacceptable. A secret with PaaS is that these costs only apply once and are shared across all users.

This also won't manage scalability. Your self-managed Jenkins instance may run on a `m1.micro` instance initially, then the growing team will require to migrate to a larger box. You will probably never get an adequate resources size, and at same time, will pay for unused resources. A PaaS that shares resources to multiple tenants lowers the costs as it enforces the best use of resources by sharing them, and adapts to your load with minimal cost.

An Amazon `m1.micro` instance, the cheaper one, cost 0.2 cents per hour. Thanks to resources sharing for a larger box with multiple users, a base RUN@cloud app-cell cost is 0.19 cents per hour, with all managed infrastructure benefits. So, a PaaS instance is cheaper than the equivalent infrastructure it offers!

For specific software stack requirement, a dedicated infrastructure can make sense sometimes, but sharing a common infrastructure allows us to reduce costs to a great extent and helps in better service. It also offers higher order automation, and the **ClickStart** options demonstrate this by providing a one-click way to set up a full project in few minutes.

Summary

This chapter demonstrated how simple it is to set up a project on the CloudBees platform. Using **ClickStart** is recommended to get started, even if you have existing code, as it will prepare a complete and working pipeline that you just have to adapt to your own project.

3
Users, Domains, and Services

As we have seen in the previous chapter, the CloudBees platform distinguishes users from the domain (also known as account, but we will avoid this confusing term).

Users and roles

The domain is created by a user and shared with other team members. You can, for example, have a domain created for your company or maybe just for a project depending on your organization. Users can then be added to the account, and the maximum user count depends on the subscription plan.

Users can have the following roles on a domain:

- **Administrators**: They can manage users and services, subscribe to services, change the subscription plan, change other users' permissions, and configure the domain to allow new users or to revoke them. There's no need to be a single administrator as there is no such notion as an *owner* of the domain.

- **Users**: They can access services but cannot change subscriptions or manage other users.

On RUN@cloud, all users can access applications and databases on the domain. Both users and administrators can create new RUN resources, application containers, or databases.

 For this reason, some companies prefer to have a distinct RUN-only production domain to host production applications and insulate the development team to a development-specific domain that can use the RUN infrastructure for testing. They then use some Jenkins-specific plugins to securely share the artifacts between accounts.

DEV@CloudForge has the same simple model. All the users can access all the resources. Repositories can be switched to public if you want to expose some open source code or distribute the artifacts via a public Maven repository.

DEV@cloud Jenkins is an exception to this minimalist role model. Thanks to the CloudBees Jenkins Enterprise plugin, **Role-based Access Control (RBAC)**, you can set up fine-grained access rules for the users on your Jenkins instance.

You can also make your Jenkins server partially public if you want to expose some build state to anonymous user, or include the build status in a wiki for sample. RBAC will then filter permissions for anonymous users compared to the official domain users.

Services

The DEV@cloud and RUN@cloud service subscriptions are managed by the Grand Central application like other services available on the CloudBees platform. Let's have a look at the **Services** management page.

This page lists the subscribed services with a link to the service and the options to change the subscription. The **Add service** button lets us explore the available services on the platform.

The following screenshot depicts the available services:

Available services

Each card on this deck shows a minimal resume of the provided service with the subscription plan fees. As you can see, most services offer a free plan, so you can test them before you consider if they actually match your requirements.

Integrated partner services

We have set up the continuous deployment in *Chapter 2*, *Getting Started Quickly*. Using a ClickStart application only uses the basic DEV and RUN services, but the CloudBees platform offers a larger set of services. They all are SaaS services that are integrated in the CloudBees platform, offering you the ability to extend your Cloud experience with additional features.

Most of them are third-party types of SaaS. CloudBees could surely host PostgreSQL or MongoDB by itself and offer it as an add-on; we actually have some of them for internal use, but as we really think of the service as a key for the Cloud adoption and not just for software automation, we prefer to let the advanced and specialized team handle them and provide all the required monitoring, maintenance, and support.

> Why does service matter so much? Cloud is generally presented from a technical perspective, but the actual paradigm shift is about switching from technology to service. When you have an issue with your Mongo database, you don't have to call a certified consultant. You can directly contact the CloudBees support, who will act as level one support and handle your issue with the MongoDB experts.

Our Jenkins instance builds our project to deploy every commit to RUN@cloud but Jenkins can do more. With Sonar, we can run code analysis on a periodic basis and measure the code's quality. Sonar being packaged as a SaaS and fully integrated in to the CloudBees platform, we only have to subscribe to this service (all it takes is a click), wait for the Sonar instance to be provisioned on Cloud servers, and then use it. CloudBees service integration manages the SSO integration, account creation on partner SaaS, and enables single billing. Subscribing to such a service is really just a one-click operation—as this is the first paying subscription we use, it will actually be more than one click as we have to enter the payment details.

Such a service integration is called "an integrated partner" in the CloudBees documentation. Integration means you don't really have to worry that the partner service is managed by a third-party company. Subscription is a one-click process that will:

- Automatically create the partner account
- Set up your CloudBees resources, install the Jenkins plugin, and declare the credentials
- Configure the billing integration so that you only get a CloudBees bill and can pay using the payment information you declared on CloudBees

The following screenshot displays the simplified subscription to an integrated partner service:

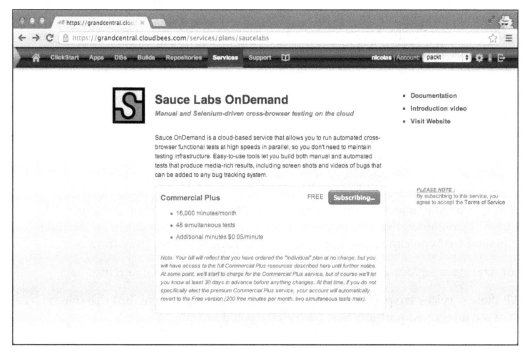

Simplified subscription to an integrated partner service

As well, we can improve our continuous integration process by running some web tests based on Selenium using real browsers provided by the SauceLabs partner. As for Sonar, CloudBees's ability to integrate will automatically manage the SaaS account creation and consolidate billing and SSO. It will also install the appropriate plugin on the Jenkins instance account and set up the credentials, so that we can set up a `selenium/saucelabs` build without having to worry about the configuration details.

There are few other services that we can use in order to improve our DEV toolbox. The JFrog'sArtifactoryMaven repository manager lets us control libraries that we can include in our application and/or release process to promote binaries. XWiki allows us to manage the development team's documentation with a very extensible wiki platform. Blazemeter can be used to run load tests on a periodic basis, so that we can detect performance regressions and fix them as soon a possible. The same model applies to RUN@cloud.

NewRelic is a monitoring and diagnostic service. It uses some application instrumentation and a runtime agent to collect metrics and provide health statistics. Thanks to the CloudBees integration, you don't have to worry about those technical details but just subscribe to this third-party service and then enable it on your application just by checking a checkbox on RUN@cloud web console. The integration service fully handles the role of setting up the appropriate agent on your application container.

PaperTrail, a SaaS log collector service, offers a comparable simplified setup experience. Just by selecting the appropriate checkbox, your application will be able to send logs to this service that will aggregate them and provide consolidation with a search interface similar to Google Search.

SendGrid offers mail services so that your application can send mails to notify your users. CloudBees integration then, in addition to consolidated authentication and billing, is used to inject the related resources into your application container. For a Java EE container, this means you'll get a JavaMail session bound into the JNDI container that you can retrieve at runtime without any extra configuration.

For data storage, MongoDB or CloudAnt can be used as NoSQL engines.

All these services are part of the so-called CloudBees ecosystem. But this one is larger than the integrated partners that we quickly listed here.

Validated partner services

The CloudBees ecosystem, mentioned in detail at `http://www.cloudbees.com/platform/ecosystem/tech-partners.cb`, includes a larger set of third-party services. Most of them aren't available on the services subscription page as they are validated partner services.

Such third-party services aren't as integrated to the CloudBees platform as Sonar or SendGrid are. CloudBees worked with such partners to agree about the commercial relations, to check whether both the services can smoothly work together, and documented the integration steps in wiki, but there is no subscription or billing integration between them.

Even the user experience is not as smooth in such integrations. The main benefit is that adding new partners to the ecosystem doesn't require any lengthy integration work. So there are more opportunities for you to get adequate services for your own use. The services that are very popular could later evolve into integrated partners.

Thanks to this model, the CloudBees ecosystem has been rapidly growing since last year. The following screenshot demonstrates the verified partner ecosystem:

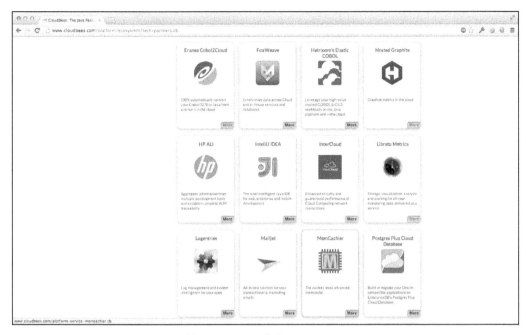

Quickly growing verified partner ecosystem

An example of why to use such a partner is for the use of database. As we've seen, CloudBees offers MySQL databases as a service on the RUN platform, but the platform users have to accept the multitenancy constraints (lack of control on advanced configuration), and are limited in the schema size up to 5 GB. For a larger database or for customization, CloudBees recommends using Amazon RDS.

The RUN team of CloudBees focuses on making the platform the best place to host the applications and doesn't want to have dedicated engineering energy focused on a **Database-as-a-Service** offer even if it makes sense to offer a simple MySQL cluster for prototyping, testing, or small general purpose databases. In actual production situations, a dedicated third-party offer makes more sense as the service provided will benefit a more specialized level of expertise, advanced configuration options, and support.

Consider the CloudBees ecosystem as a SaaS marketplace where CloudBees offers the generic platform and SaaS partners add services to it. Depending on your own use, design, development language, and practices; some of them won't make sense to you whereas some will be a requirement. Thanks to this extensibility and modularity, you can select the adequate environment for your development team and application.

Summary

This chapter demonstrated how the CloudBees platform integrates with a larger ecosystem that lets you select the adequate components to match your own requirements. This extensibility makes the platform an attractive place for software developers as they can quickly test the technologies with expert partners to manage infrastructure and services.

4
ClickStart in Depth

In *Chapter 2, Getting Started Quickly*, we used ClickStart to get an application deployed on the CloudBees platform without spending much time on the details. Let's now look further into ClickStart and learn how to use them for our own projects.

What's a ClickStart?

As you log in to the CloudBees platform, you can see a set of links on the CloudBees toolbar. The **ClickStart** link is next to the Home button. ClickStarts are a major component of the CloudBees platform, as they provide the glue between services to provide a smooth user experience.

Let's use a concrete example. Click on the **ClickStart** button to get a list of the available ClickStarts. The following screenshot shows the ClickStart selection wizard:

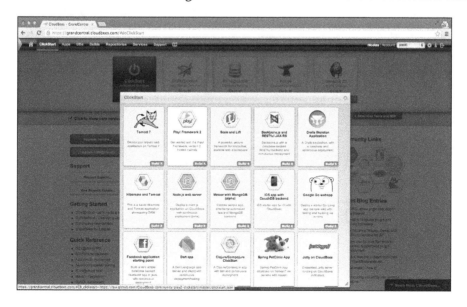

As you can see in the preceding screenshot, the CloudBees platform doesn't just support Java, but also a large set of runtimes. You will find the following in this list:

- Some JavaEE containers such as Tomcat, JBoss, Glassfish, and Jetty
- Some alternative languages and web frameworks such as Grails, Scala and Lift, and Play! Framework
- Some non-Java stacks such as Node.js, Google Go, Dart, and Erlang Webmachine
- Some more specific ClickStarts such as the iOS mobile web application and the Facebook application

Some ClickStarts such as PetClinic are pure demonstrations for the purpose of implementing the framework's blueprint on CloudBees. You can use them as an educational ClickStart to check how the configuration is set and mimic it in your own projects. Other ClickStarts are actual application skeletons to start a new project.

Let's use a Play2 ClickStart as an example in this chapter. The parameters required to launch a ClickStart are limited to giving a name to the application, as shown in the following screenshot. Everything else is managed by ClickStart. This one also checks for platform prerequisites, for example, there will be a warning if you don't have a DEV@cloud Jenkins subscription. The following screenshot displays ClickStart–a single parameter to set up a full application:

This ClickStart created the following:

- An application skeleton code, stored in a Git repository
- A Jenkins job to build and deploy the application
- An application container for the application (a Java container for a Play2 application)
- A database to store data according to the application skeleton (some ClickStarts don't use a database)

Getting the code

You can retrieve the code as you can for any other Git repository. This is just a basic application skeleton source code committed as an initial commit, as shown in the following screenshot:

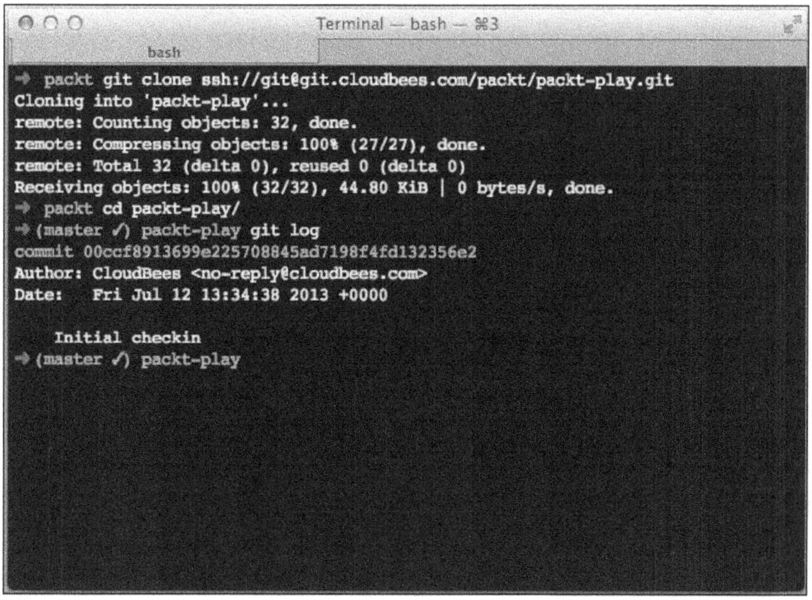

You may not be experienced in using Git as the source code management tool, but don't worry too much. Using your favorite IDE, you can make the best use of the assistance wizard to access the repository and retrieve the code. Anyway, this may be a good opportunity for you to learn using Git, and then you'll hardly use another tool.

The application generated by ClickStart is very basic and doesn't offer an advanced UI design but just demonstrates a working codebase, as shown in the following screenshot:

You can now customize the skeleton source code to demonstrate your developer's skill and convert this basic application into an awesome UI with great features and services.

Building the project

Depending on the ClickStart you choose, the created project may use various tools. Play2 uses **Scala SBT**. A Jenkins job has been generated to match this requirement. You can customize your Jenkins job, if required, to tweak the build and match your own requirements.

The following screenshot demonstrates Jenkins job configured by ClickStart:

The things to note in the generated Jenkins job are as follows:

- A forge trigger will be set to start a build when you commit some changes. Thanks to this trigger, you'll get continuous feedback on integration few minutes after a commit is pushed to the forge repository and can retrieve the built binaries.

- The CloudBees deployer will be set to deploy the built application to **RUN@cloud** when the build is successful. If your commit is valid, you'll get the associated application up and running on your PaaS in a few minutes.

Jenkins is very flexible and provides a bunch of plugins so you can customize your build in many ways. We will look into those options later in *Chapter 5, Managing Your Build*.

Managing the deployed application

The RUN@cloud web UI lets you manage your application by selecting the deployment options. Many advanced options are only available with the CloudBees SDK, which will be covered in *Chapter 7, Tools*.

The RUN@cloud web UI also lets you access the application logs (both the system output stream and the access logs), as shown in the following screenshot. They will be your best friends if you have to diagnose a deployment error. So, remember to instrument your application with debug logs and metrics.

The ClickStart ecosytem

Most ClickStarts you can see on the CloudBees UI are developed in the **CloudBees-community** GitHub account. This account has been set so you can contribute your fixes/improvements, just fork a repo, make a change, give it a try, and create a pull request.

A ClickStart, technically speaking, is a simple JSON file. Let's have a look at one of the CloudBees' ClickStarts, for example, Play2. The following screenshot demonstrates ClickStart hosted on GitHub:

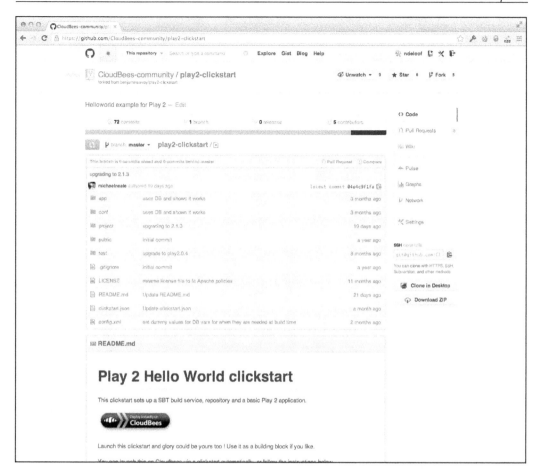

The README.md file is common in GitHub repositories, but it makes more sense here as it's the simplest way to let another user test your ClickStart, as the **Deploy Instantly on CloudBees** button suggests. All the ClickStart mechanisms are based on calling a Grand Central specific URL with a path to the ClickStart's JSON file: https://grandcentral.cloudbees.com/?CB_clickstart=<clickstart.json-URL>

The Clickstart.json file describes the requirements and resources to be generated, as shown in the following code snippet:

```
{
  "id": "play2",
  "name": "Play! Framework 2",
  "source": "github",
  "description" : "Get started with the Play Framework, version
    2, hosted natively",
```

```
    "icon" : "https://d3ko533tu1ozfq.cloudfront.net/
       clickstart/play2_icon.png",
    "supported-by" : "cloudbees",
    "order" : 1,
    "runtime": {
      "type": "play2",
      "app-parameters" : {
      "runtime.java_version": "1.7"
    }
    "app-variables":{
      "proxyBuffering":false,
      "http_version":"1.1"
    }
  },
  "build-with-jenkins": {
      "template": {
        "type": "https://raw.github.com/CloudBees-community/play2-
           clickstart/master/jenkins.xml"
      }
  }
```

The first part describes the ClickStart and its integration in the CloudBees UI (icon, documentation, and so on).

The `runtime` section describes the generated application on RUN@cloud. The container `type` is set to `play2`; refer to *Chapter 6, Running Your Applications*, and *Chapter 8, Using ClickStack to Extend the Platform*, for more details on runtime containers.

Build is defined as a Jenkins job based on a `Jenkins config.xml` export file. Some tokens are used to replace the fragments with the information provided when the ClickStart is executed, such as a Git repository URL and an application, and the account name.

Nothing more! It is very simple, and you can quickly build your own ClickStart.

Writing your own ClickStart

ClickStart is such a simple way to set up a project but you will probably have to write few of them for your own projects. You can use them to prepare a project skeleton, enforcing all the best practices in development stage when the project is bootstrapped.

Let's create a ClickStart from scratch. We'll illustrate this by setting up a ClickStart for SimpleWeb4J, a lightweight REST-based web framework, which was recently created by my friend, Yan.

First, create a new GitHub repository to host our ClickStart. For simplicity, this one will also host the codebase for the app to be deployed. The project skeleton is basically a `maven pom.xml` file and comprises few classes.

Let's then create an adequate Jenkins job to build this project and produce a `jar` file with the application ready to be deployed, including all of its dependencies. In the next chapter, we will cover how to use Jenkins to set up a job in more detail; anyway, this isn't a complex task. Now we need to perform the following:

- Create a Maven job
- Configure an adequate Git repository and some Maven goals
- Configure the post-build deployment to RUN@cloud

Now let's export this job as an XML file using the JOB_URL/config.xml URL. We just need to replace the Git repository URL with ${repositoryUrl}; similarly, for ${account} and ${application} to get the jenkins.xml template added to our ClickStart repository.

Last but not least, we have to write the clickstart.json file for this new ClickStart, as shown in the following code snippet:

```
{
    "id": "simpleweb4j-clickstart",
    "name": "SimpleWeb4j",
    "source": "github",
    "description" : "SimpleWeb4j application in continuous
      deployment",
    "icon" : "https://raw.github.com/ndeloof/simpleweb4j-
      clickstart/master/icon.png",
    "supported-by" : "community",
    "runtime": {
      "type": "java",
      "app-parameters" : {
        "runtime.class": "com.mycompany.Main"
      }
    },
    "build-with-jenkins": {
      "template": {
      "type": "https://raw.github.com/ndeloof/simpleweb4j-
        clickstart/master/jenkins.xml",
      }
    }
}
```

Just add a README.md file with an adequate link and push the resulting project to GitHub. We're done! We can now test our new ClickStart (shown screenshot available at https://github.com/ndeloof/simpleweb4j-clickstart) and share the link with our friends. The following screenshot demonstrates how to use ClickStart to promote your own projects:

Summary

This chapter demonstrated how CloudBees' ClickStart lets you bootstrap a project in few seconds, and how you can easily set up your own ClickStart for your own frameworks, development rules, and practices. We expect the ClickStart ecosystem to quickly grow and provide a large set of templates for various frameworks and application architectures.

5
Managing Your Build

The ClickStart application generated a build job, so we didn't look further into the Jenkins **Continuous Integration** (**CI**) server and the way it has been tweaked as a Cloud-hosted service called DEV@cloud. Let's get into the details now.

Jenkins

Formerly known as Hudson, Jenkins is the de facto standard for the CI server in the Java ecosystem, and is also becoming popular in other communities. Its primary task is continuous integration. It checks project health on a regular basis using automated build and test scripts. Jenkins offers an extensible design and is based on the plugin, so that it can offer a simplified UI or specialized features for some specific use cases.

Continuous Integration

Integration used to be a project management phase, which gets started after the code development has been completed, to put the software components together and pass some tests to ensure that the project goals are achieved. This used to be complex, time consuming, and used to reveal bugs that had a huge impact on codebase because they had been detected late.

As an Agile software development evangelist said, "If it hurts too much, do it more, on smaller assets", so Extreme Programming has promoted CI. The principle of CI is to run the integration phase as much as possible (at least once a day) so that you can have a quick feedback on the code change impacts and revert or fix them quickly at limited costs.

Automation

Running the integration phase during all the development process can't be achieved by a human test team, as this would not only be a huge effort and a high cost, but it will also be a repetitive. This means that doing it manually is not the best option. Automating the build, test, and packaging process is the basis for continuous practices. Thanks to the advanced build tools, test frameworks, embeddable application containers, and advanced deployment managers, software development project can fully automate the integration process nowadays. Jenkins offers to run it on a regular basis (this can be for every commit) and produce reports for the developers to have a constant feedback on project health.

Jenkins is not restricted to continuous integration. Being based on a high-level abstraction and relying on plugins for all specific tasks, it can be used to manage a large set of automations, software development and management tasks, reporting, and more.

Extensibility

Jenkins architecture is specifically designed for extensibility and to define a set of extension points. This allows features of Jenkins to be segregated into dedicated plugins, each of them hosted on a dedicated repository in GitHub. This *divide and conquer* strategy lets the Jenkins open source community grow quickly, with the contributors being focused on small subsets.

Jenkins open source community maintains more than 650 plugins. They cover all the aspects of software development and automation such as SCM support, build and test tool integration, deployment management, reporting and notification, and build orchestration.

Scalability

Jenkins runs as a monolithic web application, but it can control a set of servers that are known as **build slaves**. Jenkins can distribute its job's execution on those slaves to limit the master load, by handling only the Web UI. This allows a Jenkins installation to be scalable up to thousands of jobs, driving hundreds of slave machines.

DEV@cloud

CloudBees, DEV@cloud offers Jenkins as a Service that is hosted in the Cloud. This can be used as a standalone SaaS; but as ClickStart demonstrated, it also fits well in the CloudBees integrated development chain.

The following screenshot shows a Jenkins instance that has been set for our CloudBees account. The ClickStart we used generated a build job, but we can define many more and even organize them into views or group them into folders. A Jenkins instance for a large company can handle thousands of jobs!

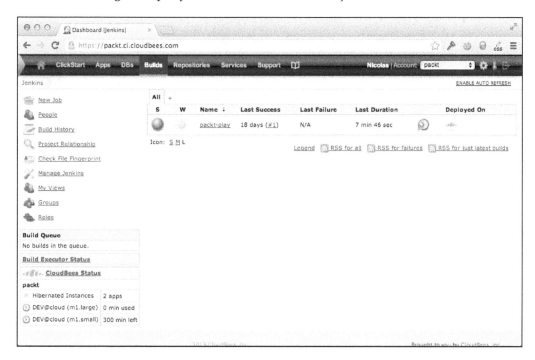

Each job defines what should be done as an automated task, and also tells when it should be done. Jenkins UI is fully web-based and offers lots of options (depending on the installed plugins), which are grouped into sections. All of them can grow depending on the installed plugins. The sections defined in the **Builds** menu are as follows:

- The main section defines the job name, parameters, and the Jenkins execution constraints (where to build and when to purge data).

- The **Source Code Management** section lets you define from where you can get the code. This reveals that Jenkins was initially designed for CI, but you can select **None** if you wish to run some periodic tasks.

- The **Build Triggers** section lets you define when to run this job. It can be based on a periodic cron (checking for SCM changes using polling, which depends on other job execution), or it can get automatically triggered when code is pushed to SCM. The latter one is the better option as you won't have any delay and you'll get a quick feedback.

- The **Build Environment** section lets you define how to set up the build before it actually starts. It can be used, for example, to expose environment variables.

- The **Build** section is used to define the actual build. Various build steps are declared here to provide the full build process. They will be run sequentially, and the sequence will stop on the first failure.

- The **Post-build Actions** section is used to collect reporting data, archive build results, and to the notify the team on build status.

The following screenshot shows the **Build Environment**, **Build**, and **Post-build Actions** sections:

Customization

Jenkins top-level **Manage** link lets you customize your Jenkins instance. The global configuration can be used, for example, to manage the installation of tools that will be exposed to job configuration. The initial configuration includes all the preinstalled JDKs available on DEV@cloud slaves, but you might not have to care about JDK 5 and might want to remove it in order to avoid the UI getting confused or software being built using this JDK by mistake. In that case, you can remove it or configure your own versions.

CloudBees provides a large set of preinstalled tools, and an autoinstaller can be used to extend the available toolset.

Plugins

DEV@cloud has a set of preinstalled plugins that allow Jenkins to run most use cases. For your own project, you will probably search for some missing features.

Also, you can access the Plugin Manager (**Jenkins | Manage | Plugins**) to select plugins that will be installed on your instance. The CloudBees update center doesn't expose the 650 plugins available in the Jenkins community, for usage simplification. It provides the most requested plugins only. If you miss a specific plugin and want it to be installed, just refer to the support process. Installing a plugin requires Jenkins to restart (UI lets you think this is optional, but I recommend you to restart Jenkins for an Eclipse plugin installation).

On-demand slaves

DEV@cloud is designed to let you benefit from Cloud-based hosting. So, your Jenkins master won't run any build on the master's host. CloudBees manages a slave pool, provisioning new slave instances when the global service load grows, based on the Amazon Web Services IaaS elasticity. As a new build starts on your Jenkins instance, the CloudBees slave pool assigns you an available slave for running your build.

 CloudBees provides both `m1.small` (default) and `m1.large` build slaves. The latter is more or less two times faster. If your project requires significant build resources (`m1.small` only has 2 GB memory) or you want to speed up a few a classic builds, you can set the **Restrict where this project can run** option to `m1.large`.

With Amazon Cloud as the sole limit to your slave allocation, you can trigger a dozen concurrent builds when required. That's a significant change in the way you consider your software factory. Now there's no reason for not triggering a build on every commit, or for not computing QA metrics on the code on a regular basis. The cost of build minutes is so low (10 cents per hour) that an on-demand build slave can be used for a large set of tasks to improve your development process.

Continuous delivery

Continuous delivery a typical improvement to CI. Applying the principle of Agile software practices, it's based on the definition of *done* for a software developer. A task is done when there's no more manual or untested steps involved in getting the related code pushed to production.

When you tell your Project Lead that you have completed development on item `#987`; in many cases, you may mean that you have done the following things:

- Developed the item
- Ran some tests
- Maybe wrote some automated tests
- Possibly asked a colleague to review your code

Is your code actually ready for production? Did you do the following:

- Compute the QA metrics to ensure that the code follows team conventions and make application look better than it was before you contributed (known as **boy scoots principle**)
- Run the deployment process in a production equivalent environment

- Run acceptance and performance tests on the application to check its impact
- Give the production team enough information so that they don't need any manual or untested process to be run

I won't blame you since the ability to embrace the whole development process up to production isn't easy, and it often hits some organization barriers. Anyway, just consider how this changes in a Cloud-based environment.

Our CI allows us as many computer resources as we need. Our server is a PaaS. We will get into more details in *Chapter 6, Running Your Applications*, but by nature, this is a fully automated, on-demand service for hosting our application.

Full chain automation – continuous deployment

The first step is to introduce you to the continuous deployment process, which you already know — thanks to ClickStart! Every commit is built, tested, and deployed to the PaaS on successful testing. Thanks to the full API-based automation in PaaS, there's no manual process involved in getting the last commit available as a running application.

For a production server, this is probably a little risky for most of us. But for a development team, this is just awesome.

- Do you need to show product owner how his/her new widget will look? Just use continuous delivery to a demo application. Discussion with product management, designers, and user experience experts will be far easier.

- Do you want to perform some acceptance or functional tests? Deploy to a test instance on PaaS using a production equivalent setup and run your tests. Kill the application after test consumption. Even for a large application, such a test will only cost few cents.

- Do you want to diagnose a bug? Deploy the last tagged version to your own test instance on the PaaS.

- Do you want to release your application to production? This is the exact same deployment process that you used for the demo app! It is just another target environment.

PaaS is a dream environment for continuous delivery evangelists. By nature, all deployments use exactly the same fully automated process. On-demand resources allow the replication of the environment for different uses, and production is just one of them — from a platform and process point of view.

Implementing this on DEV@cloud Jenkins is easy. You only need to clone the job definition and application container. Jenkins even offers a **Copy from** option, as shown in the following screenshot, while creating a new job that will make this trivial.

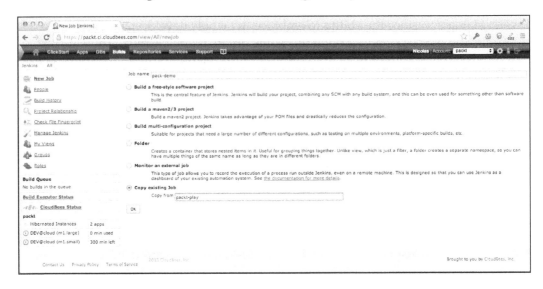

We now just have to configure the production job to monitor a distinct production branch, and configure our demo job to monitor the master branch. With such a setup, deploying to production is just a Git merge operation.

Job chain

Maybe you don't like the option of getting the production deployment process to be based on a Git merge. This is well accepted by the developers who don't use a compiled language, as the deployed artifact is more or less just the source code packaged in some way. As such, Java developers are not confident with the build process for generating a reproducible binary.

If you prefer the production deployment to use the exact same binary package that you deployed for development, you can chain the Jenkins job together. As some phone device company would say, "There's a plugin for this."

When Jenkins runs a job, the resulting artifact(s) can be archived on Jenkins master for later use. This is controlled by a post-build action. Maven jobs automatically archive the produced Maven artifacts, so this is even simpler.

After a job has been completed, you can trigger another one automatically as a downstream job using the **Build another project** post-build action. This can be useful if you want your CI job to report compilation and unit test failure quickly, and trigger a longer functional testing suite on success. The job to manage this test suite will reuse the previously built artifact; deploy it to a test server on the PaaS, run the tests, and shut down the resources. For this purpose, the Copy Artifact plugin can be used, which is configured to retrieve an artifact from the upstream build that triggered this job. The following screenshot depicts the options in the **Builds** window:

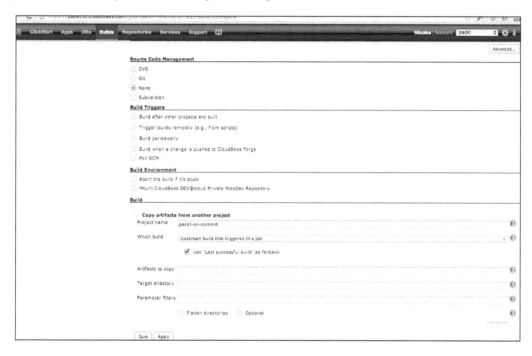

With such a setup, every commit will be tested by the on-commit job; and then all successful commits will be tested by the functional test suite. We can then follow up with the other jobs to run performance tests, compute QA metrics, and so on.

Promotion

Jenkins' promoted builds plugin is another plugin that can help in this scenario. This plugin allows the tagging of a build based on some criteria and gets some actions executed when this promotion occurs.

A typical use of this plugin is to have a nightly performance job to stress test the application, and ensure that the latest development didn't introduce performance regressions. This job needs artifacts from the previous day that passed all the test chains successfully. So, we need some way to know which on-commit builds were both successful and passed the functional test suite.

Promotion can be used here to tag a build when downstream functional suite is successful as well. It will detect the success of downstream job and add a visual flag on the build history. We can re-use this information from another performance job to make the Copy Artifact plugin use the last promoted build as the source for artifact. The following screenshot shows the **Promotion process** window:

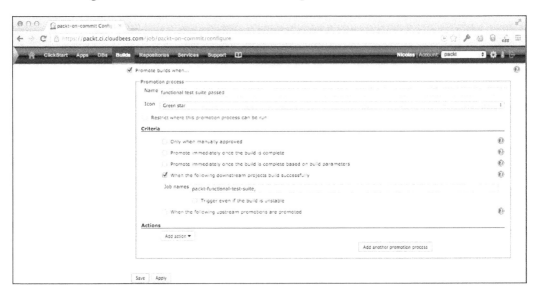

Promotion plugin can also run some actions when the promotion occurs. We can use this to create a manual promotion. Compared to the one we've seen so far, this one has no criteria but just waits for some approved user to click on the **Approve** button. The associated action will use the same deployment process that we used a dozen times during development, but it will be configured for the production environment.

Summary

This chapter demonstrated how the extensible Jenkins server lets us define a simple but powerful job chain. We quickly demonstrated two plugins, but the large ecosystem offers incredible options to improve the Jenkins' capability in order to embrace your own development process. Combined with the PaaS deployment, API simplicity, and flexibility, Jenkins with the Cloud-based unlimited resources offers great opportunities for your development team to introduce new testing tools and implement the best development practices.

6
Running Your Applications

In the previous chapter, we set up Jenkins to deploy our application for various development and production scenarios. Let's now get deeper into the RUN@cloud platform and its features.

Scalability

Talking about Cloud to host your application, we're comparing to classic hardware. Such servers are large memory—high-CPU computers in a self-hosted datacenter. Many applications, even the high-load ones, running in such a context are monolithic, single-server applications. The Cloud is based on smaller low-cost machines, which are available by dozen when necessary.

Vertical scalability is the option to *scale up* the application to a larger server when it requires more resources. This makes sense in the Cloud context as the on-demand resources and automated APIs let you restart your application on a new server within minutes. So, you can use a larger server as your application load grows, but keep in mind that there's a limit. Let's consider the features of Amazon EC2 `m1.large` computer:

- 64 bits CPU 4 compute unit (this is equivalent to a 4 Intel Xeon 2007 1 GHz CPU)
- 7.5 GB memory
- 800 GB ephemeral disk
- Moderate network performance

Such a large server is comparable to the MacBook pro I'm using to write this chapter. For sure, EC2 provides larger virtual instances, but you have to remember that you can't keep a monolithic application model in mind, or you will hit a wall when the application will have to serve a larger traffic.

On CloudBees' RUN@cloud application server, you can select the application to use from one up to eight **app-cells**, app-cell being a server slice. Depending on your application usage, you can then adjust to the exact resource consumption and lower costs, as you can see in the following screenshot:

Application container selection

Horizontal scalability

You can't get a super-large server, but you can get a dozen of them if required. **Clustering** is a solution for scalability issues, which the software architects have known for a while. With small low-cost machines, the Cloud offers you an opportunity to adjust your resources to the actual application load, as long as your application has been well designed for a clustered environment. This has some architectural constraints, which we will explore further in this chapter.

On the RUN@cloud web UI, you can select the number of nodes you want your application to be deployed to. So you can, for example, get the application running on three servers using two app-cells on each of them. The ability to adjust resources is nice, but it would be even better if you don't have to manage it by yourself! The **Automatic Scaling** option, as shown in the following screenshot, lets you define some metrics for the platform, to add a node to your cluster or to remove one:

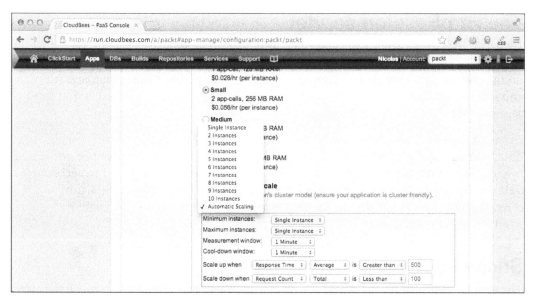

Application autoscaling configuration

You just have to define the boundaries for auto-scaling, and accordingly the platform will adjust the resources to your actual application load.

Clustering constraints

Running your application in a clustered mode introduces some constraints. They aren't cloud-specific, but developers may not be familiar with them.

State

The main issue with clustering is **state**. As your application runs on a set of nodes, and you have subsequent requests from user to build a *conversation*, a distinct node may handle some of them. How can node B access the shopping cart that the customer has populated when server A handled his first request?

Cloud evangelists suggest the idea of being **stateless**. A stateless world would be cool for software architects as this would make distributed software far simpler. There are many ways the state can be managed in an application.

The HttpSession servlet

Using the API **HttpSession** servlet is a common implementation in the Java ecosystem, relying on the JavaEE container to manage the replication of the session on the cluster. The specification doesn't detail anything about the implementation, and lets the vendor provide innovative solutions. The sole requirement is that the session data should be serializable.

By using the session store option to set up a distributed cache for storing session data, you can use HttpSession on CloudBees as well. The session store is a dedicated memcache bound to your application's node on the cluster. Compared to serializing data on disk or a database, a memcache is pretty quick to distribute data, and offers a nice solution to migrate existing applications to the cloud and benefit from immediate scalability.

Sticky session

The session store sometime isn't enough, and you need to *degrade* cluster elasticity by using sticky sessions (**session affinity**).

SDK offers the `stickySession=true` option when deploying an application, such that a user will always use the exact same server. The drawback is that the load can't be fully distributed on the cluster, and when a node is removed, the associated users will lose their session.

The use of a sticky session versus a session store is a question of the application's business model. If you don't care about the few users who might experience slowness or have to create a new session when an application is redeployed, a sticky session will let you migrate your good old servlet-based application to CloudBees without the extra cost of a session store. This can also be a temporary solution, waiting for some architectural improvement.

 Beware of your frameworks! Sometimes your code is perfectly stateless and may not require a sticky session, but the frameworks you're using can introduce some obstacles. A typical example is grails, security plugin. This one uses spring security with default settings which relies on HttpSession. This can be fixed by some advanced configurations, but a developer to enable the plugin as a one-liner security solution probably don't expect this.

The client-side state

Play framework and a few other stateless web frameworks use HTTP cookies so that the user maintains the state in his browser. The server doesn't manage any state between requests and only relies on cookies to get the current conversation.

This seems a good option, but be careful with state weight. If you need a dozen kilobytes of cookies to maintain the state, all your application requests, including static resources and AJAX calls will include these cookies, and this will lower the application's performance from a user's point of view, but the server doesn't suffer from traffic load.

So, the common recommendation is to just set the minimal state, transferring only IDs, and not details. Then you have to pay for the underlying extra cost to retrieve data on every request, and it will need caching. After this, you will need synchronization and then some sort of state management.

Things are easier with an immutable domain model, as there's no need for cache synchronization anymore, but you pay for more write operations.

As a resume, the full client-side state is probably the cleaner architecture, but has some significant architecture impacts for a high-load application.

> *"Be stateless as much as you can."*

I used to say this as it is a question of compromise between stateless services, HTTP weight, data immutability, and adequate cache management. Some web frameworks and data store engines help you to implement this.

The ephemeral filesystem

The filesystem is some sort of state you have to worry about in a clustered or Cloud environment. By nature, a filesystem is local to the node that is partially running an application on the cluster group. If you use a filesystem to store user uploads and then compute into an internal application model, everything is fine, but if you use it for persistent data, you will loose some data.

You know that every request can be handled by a distinct node on the cluster, but you also have to know that the application redeployment will start on a fresh set of nodes, so previously stored data on the filesystem will be lost. This is known as an **ephemeral filesystem** — the opposite to a persistent filesystem.

The Cloud provider, Google App Engine, just forbids the access to the Java File API. CloudBees doesn't consider the filesystem to be evil, but it just has to be used in the appropriate way.

A persistent filesystem has major drawbacks, both with performance and locking constraints. When required by application model, CloudBees provides an optional add-on to use Amazon S3 as a persistent file store, mounted as a local directory. This isn't a silver bullet solution as performances and delayed write behavior on S3 to a local filesystem. Anyway, this can help you migrate your application to the Cloud.

As a long-term solution, using a file store explicitly is the best option. The benefit is that you'll have to consider the filesystem use case—is the data temporary or really persistent? Does it make sense for it to be stored in a database, as a BLOB? For actual file store access, I recommend the JClouds API, which offers a neutral frontend on file store service, and a local filesystem option that you can enable during development or debugging.

So far, we've mostly seen constraints introduced by cloud-based application hosting, and with a proposed workaround and solution, now you may consider scalability as a limited added value for you to pay all required refactoring. So, let's see some more pleasant features.

Customizing the domain

Your deployed application is available as `http://<appId>.<accountName>.cloudbees.net`. This is fine for prototyping or test application, but you probably want to display your website to users with a better URL.

Mapping your domain name

For mapping your domain name, the first thing to do is to buy a domain name. Although CloudBees doesn't provide this service, there are dozens of registrars available. To select one, just consider that you don't need any hosting option, as this is a common value-added service they offer, and instead need fine-grained control over your DNS.

As you get a domain name, you just have to configure your DNS settings (the way to do this depends on your registrar) to declare `www.yourdomain.com` as a CNAME to `appId.accountName.cloudbees.net`.

 Maybe you want to use a naked domain, that is, let the user access your web application without the `www.` prefix? Some registrars offer an auto-redirect option to www. Another solution is to define an *A* DNS entry to point to an HTTP router IP. To know the IP to be used ,run the command `ping <appId>.<accountName>.cloudbees.net`.

Please note that DNS propagation may take some hours (up to a day), so you may not see your application responding to the expected URL, but other users can see this—including CloudBees support agents. You only need to wait for the DNS servers to sync around the world.

SSL encryption

To improve application security, using HTTPS is a minimal improvement to introduce into your application. Please note that you need a dedicated domain for this option.

 You first need to buy an SSL certificate for your domain. If possible, select a wildcard certificate that will cover all subdomains of .yourcompany.com, so that you can use the same for all deployed applications on CloudBees without extra cost.

On CloudBees RUN@cloud, this is about setting up a dedicated SSL router to serve HTTP traffic to your application. This one will act as a reverse proxy, handling the secured SSL connection with a browser and translating into a standard HTTP connection to your application container.

You have to use the CloudBees SDK to set up the SSL router as there's no UI for this advanced operation. We will further describe the SDK in *Chapter 7, Tools*.

The certificate file has to use a Nginx format and should include all the certificates up to the root certificate, in child-parent order. As a text file, this is just about concatenating the certificate files together. SDK lets you validate your certificate to ensure everything is ok by using the following command:

```
beesapp:cert:validate -a ACCOUNT -cert FILE -pkPRIVATE_KEY
```

After validation, you can create a dedicated router using the following:

```
beesapp:router:create -a ACCOUNT/APP -cert FILE -pk PRIVATE_KEY myrouter
Resource: account/myrouter
config:
  SSL=true
  ROUTER_SERVICE=account-abcdef99.revproxy
  ROUTER_URL=https://99.99.192.123
```

Router is now ready to handle incoming HTTPS traffic for your application. You now have to configure your DNS to translate the application domain into your dedicated router IP as an *A* record. Due to the DNS propagation delay, this will take few hours, so we recommend you set up SSL and the domain name together if you plan to deliver a public service.

Your router will serve both HTTP and HTTPS traffic. For web resources that require secure access, your application has to check the X-Forwarded-Proto HTTP header for incoming requests to be set to HTTPS. Modern security frameworks support this de-facto standard header.

The private mode

Your application may not be designed for public use, and by nature, a Cloud platform is accessible from any Internet connection. This is also the case for your development and test instances that you only want the team members to have access to.

The private mode is a platform option that you can enable to inject a security filter in the HTTP traffic chain. The actual implementation depends on the runtime you selected for your application and this option may even not be available (see later in this chapter). Using the private mode protects your application with a credentials-based authentication, without any requirement to tweak your own code or configuration.

As we've seen in *Chapter 5, Managing Your Build*, continuous delivery only makes sense if the production deployment is the exact same process that developers use on a daily basis for (automated) testing. With the private mode, your application is safe from external users, but can be deployed to production as is for public service.

Monitoring

Most Java developers don't have a DevOps culture. Anyway, when your core service application is running, you need its health to be checked.

As a **Platform as a Service (PaaS)**, CloudBees monitors the infrastructure and platform runtime, but can't get into the specific details for your application. CloudBees' platform automation will detect memory overconsumption and kill the server, starting a new one, but it can't diagnose the cause of the problem.

The CloudBees ecosystem includes a set of production services to instrument your application. NewRelic and AppDynamics will inject probes into your application and extract the internal state into a monitoring dashboard. With some customizations, you can improve data extraction to get a relevant health report for your application.

PaperTrail is a distributed logging aggregator. In a clustered context, as all nodes have their own log, it allows you to sync all of them in a single console and have a consolidated view on application state.

Those services will offer runtime-level metrics, but you can also instrument your application to generate business metrics, and export them from your application into a dedicated dashboard. HostedGraphite hosts a Graphite graph and query engine for you. With adequate business data exported, you can compute useful graphs for your business management on real-time application metrics.

ClickStack

CloudBees claims to be *the Java PaaS company*, and even RUN@cloud focuses on providing a first-class Java Cloud service first, though it can host other runtimes.

The RUN@cloud application runtime is defined by a ClickStack (don't confuse with the **ClickStart** options). The RUN@cloud core service **GenApp** is an **Erlang** execution engine that starts ClickStacks, and displays application metadata and configuration parameters. ClickStack is responsible for installing and setting up the runtime environment, preparing the application, and starting the runtime process.

We will discuss ClickStack in detail in *Chapter 8, Using ClickStack to Extend the Platform*, you just have to know they aren't limited to running a JVM. The CloudBees community GitHub account offers a large set of runtime ClickStacks contributed both by CloudBees engineering staff and customers, as you can see in the following screenshot:

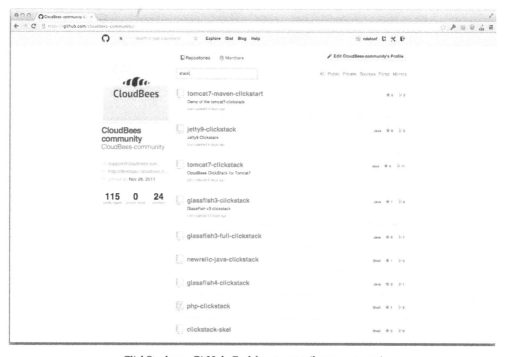

ClickStacks on GitHub. Feel free to contribute your own!

Most of these ClickStacks offer various Java containers, but there's also PHP, Node. js, or Dart ClickStack, which you can use. Thanks to ClickStack, if you have some custom requirement, running on a PaaS isn't a limitation, and you can fork the official one to add your own tweaks.

You just have to be aware that the features we've seen in this chapter are only fully available on few ClickStacks (Tomcat 6 and JBoss 7 at this time, Tomcat 7 is about to be completed).

Summary

This chapter demonstrated the RUN@cloud PaaS capability to host the application with advanced scalability and features to help in migrating to the Cloud. We had a quick overview on ClickStack, which will be discussed further in *Chapter 8, Using ClickStack to Extend the Platform*, but you already understand how flexible the RUN@cloud platform is, thanks to this extensible model.

7
Tools

The preceding chapters were mostly based on CloudBees web UI, but for actual development you need more flexible tools and integrating it in your developer's toolbox. CloudBees provides a set of tools for this purpose:

- A **Software Development Kit (SDK)** that you can use to control your RUN@cloud applications
- An Eclipse plugin for full integration with the most used IDE (considering the best one is another debate)

CloudBees SDK

CloudBees SDK is an extensible command-line tool to manage CloudBees resources and services. Compared to web UI, it lets you manage all the advanced features for the CloudBees services, so it will quickly be necessary for you to manage your CloudBees applications.

Installation

You can download CloudBees SDK from `http://wiki.cloudbees.com/bin/view/RUN/BeesSDK`. This is a simple multiplatform ZIP file you can uncompress and then add the exploded path to your system path.

Mac users can also install CloudBees as a homebrew package using the command `brew install cloudbees-sdk`.

Then, run the `bees init` command and provide user credentials for SDK to set up your $HOME/.bees directory, and install the initial plugins as shown in the following screenshot:

```
000                   Terminal — bash — ⌘3
                bash
⇥ ~ brew install cloudbees-sdk
⇒ Downloading http://cloudbees-downloads.s3.amazonaws.com/sdk/cloudbees-sdk-1.
Already downloaded: /Library/Caches/Homebrew/cloudbees-sdk-1.5.0.zip
🍺 /usr/local/Cellar/cloudbees-sdk/1.5.0: 264 files, 7,9M, built in 2 seconds
⇥ ~ bees init
Updating Bees SDK. This may take a while

You have not created a CloudBees configuration profile, let's create one now...
Enter your default CloudBees API end point [us | eu]: eu
Enter your CloudBees account email address: nicolas.deloof+packt@gmail.com
Enter your CloudBees account password:
Downloading CloudBees SDK configuration from http://cloudbees-downloads.s3.amazo
naws.com/sdk/cloudbees-sdk-config-5.xml
.
download completed
Installing plugin: org.cloudbees.sdk.plugins:ant-plugin:1.3.0
Plugin installed: org.cloudbees.sdk.plugins:ant-plugin:1.3.0
Installing plugin: org.cloudbees.sdk.plugins:app-plugin:1.5.2
Plugin installed: org.cloudbees.sdk.plugins:app-plugin:1.5.2
Installing plugin: org.cloudbees.sdk.plugins:config-plugin:1.3.2
Plugin installed: org.cloudbees.sdk.plugins:config-plugin:1.3.2
Installing plugin: org.cloudbees.sdk.plugins:db-plugin:1.3.2
Plugin installed: org.cloudbees.sdk.plugins:db-plugin:1.3.2
Installing plugin: com.cloudbees.sdk.plugins:service-plugin:1.2.2
Plugin installed: com.cloudbees.sdk.plugins:service-plugin:1.2.2
⇥ ~
```

 CloudBees SDK uses plugins to provide commands. This extensible architecture allows engineering to provide additional features, such as the blue-green plugin we will experiment with later in this chapter, as well as technology partners that provide specific commands that will fully integrate within SDK.

Basic usage

SDK provides commands to list and manage your resources. It runs `bees` without parameters for a list of available commands. Let's illustrate this with some samples.

The following commands give you a list of deployed applications:

```
⇥  ~ bees app:list
```

Application	Status	URL	Instance(s)
packt/packt	active	packt.packt.cloudbees.net	1
packt/packt-play	hibernate	packt-play.packt.cloudbees.net	1

The previous commands display all applications for our accounts (as set initially by the `bees init` command) with the current status and number of nodes on a cluster. The `Packt/packt-play` application was *hibernated* and automatically stopped as this is a free application that was inactive for hours.

Let's retrieve more information on the `packt` application:

```
➜   ~ bees app:info -a packt/packt
Application     : packt/packt
Title           : packt/packt
Created         : Thu May 16 14:50:52 CEST 2013
Status          : active
URL             : packt.packt.cloudbees.net
clusterSize     : 1
container       : java_tiny
containerType   : tomcat7
idleTimeout     : -1
maxMemory       : 128
proxyBuffering  : false
securityMode    : PUBLIC
serverPool      : stax-global (Stax Global Pool)
```

Let's distribute this application over three nodes:

```
➜   ~ bees app:scale -a packt/packt -up 2
application - packt/packt: scaled up to 3
```

Then stop the app as follows:

```
➜     ~ bees app:stop -a packt/packt
Are you sure you want to stop this application [packt/packt]: (y/n) y
application stopped - packt/packt
```

 The application has been stopped, not deleted. If we use SDK to restart the application now, it will start on three nodes on the cluster as previously configured. Remember this principle: a configuration set by SDK is for an application, not for a specific instance running on the cluster, and will survive a restart.

Runtime parameters

SDK lets you customize the container running your application. For this purpose, you use either the `app:deploy` command or the `app:update` command. The former creates and deploys a new application, while the latter updates an existing application, but both accept the same parameters as explained in the following list:

- `containerSize` lets you control the size (app-cells) for the container to host your application. The default value is free, and you can configure the size across small (one app-cell), medium, large, and extra large (eight app-cells).

- `jvmPermSize` lets you control the `XX:MaxPermSize` option, which is required for some web frameworks to generate many dynamic classes, such as Grails.

- `httpVersion` lets you configure the protocol used to connect reverse proxy to your application. It has to be set at `1.1` to support WebSockets.

- `jvmTimeZone` and `jvmFileEncoding` let you tweak the JVM localization parameters. They default to **GMT/UTC** and **UTF-8**.

As you can see, some of these parameters are generic while others are specific to JVM-based runtime. Setting `jvmPermSize` won't have any impact on a Node.js application. As Java was the first runtime implemented by CloudBees, SDK does include some JVM-specific parameters, but with the ClickStack extensible architecture, stack-specific parameters are now set by runtime parameters using the `-R` option.

For example, we can change the JRE used to run application to Java 8 (early access as I'm writing this book; it will be very useful to check if your application is compliant with Java 8 and possible regressions):

```
➜  ~ bees app:update -R java_version=1.8 -a packt/packt
This command will restart your application, are you sure you want to
update this application [packt/packt]: (y/n) y

application - packt/packt updated: ok - restarted
```

Customizing your application

If you are familiar with the JavaEE model, you will know that JNDI was designed for application customization, assuming that the container would provide some way to configure injected parameters (strings) and resources. However, this never proved to be a good model, and most developers used to have some external properties file, system properties, or a comparable hack to inject values into the application and manage values at runtime depending on the environment.

Generally speaking, all frameworks used to offer some configuration facilities based on environment variables or system properties (in the Java ecosystem).

Application parameters

Application parameters are the CloudBees mechanism to customize the runtime of an application without changing the deployed artifact. As you use SDK to define an application parameter, this one is tied to the application ID and injected as an environment variable and/or a system property.

Application parameters are managed using the `config:*` command group `config:set` lets you define a parameter and value; while `config:list` lets you review the actual values. We can, for example, set the publication date for the application to `2014`:

➜ ~ bees config:set -a packt/packt -P publication=2014
Application config parameters for packt/packt: saved

Application Parameters:
publication=2014
Runtime Parameters:
  java_version=1.8

From the preceding application code, I can retrieve this value as a Java system property:

```
System.getProperty("publication")
```

The value will change depending on whether we redeploy the application or change the configuration. I also can deploy the same WAR archive using a distinct application ID and set another value for exactly the same parameter:

➜ ~ bees app:deploy -P publication=2013 -a packt/packt-optimistic packt.war
Deploying application packt/packt-optimistic (environment:): packt.war
Config parameters: {publication=2013}

...

A common usage of this is to define application's configuration as system properties (most frameworks do support the replacement of system properties in configuration files), and deploy exactly the same application in distinct environments (development, test, staging, or production) with a distinct value set.

Resource management and binding

Injecting system properties is nice, but real-world applications rely not just on string parameters, but also on external resources. You can for sure inject the database URL and credentials and manage the connection within your own code, but for a Java EE application, you might probably prefer using a connection pool injected as a `javax.jdbc.DataSource` feature.

Resource binding is the mechanism used on CloudBees to tie other resources on your account to your application and let the container expose them using the appropriate API.

Let's first create a database. We used to browse the web UI for such operations, but we can use SDK to get exactly the same result:

```
➜  ~ bees db:create -a packt packt-db
Database Username (must be unique): packt-db
Database Password: packt-db
database created: packt-db
```

Let's now bind this (newly created) database to our application. This is a simple SDK command:

```
bees app:bind -a packt/packt -db packt/packt-db -as PacktDB
```

After restart or redeployment, the application will have a `PacktDb` (as defined by alias) DataSource available in JNDI. With appropriate `<resource-ref>` objects declared in `WEB-INF/web.xml`, we can retrieve it from our application code as we would for any other Java EE compliant container:

```
<resource-ref>
      <description>DataSource for CloudBees DB</description>
      <res-ref-name>jdbc/PacktDB</res-ref-name>
      <res-type>javax.sql.DataSource</res-type>
      <res-auth>Container</res-auth>
</resource-ref>

InitialContext ctx = new InitialContext();
DataSource ds = (DataSource) ctx.lookup("java:/comp/env/jdbc/
PacktDB");
```

Plugins

So far, we only have seen some `app:*`, `db:*`, and `config:*` commands, but running bees without parameters to get an available command list confirms that there is a lot more. The commands are grouped and distributed into plugins you can manage using the `plugin:*` commands:

```
→    ~ bees plugin:list
# CloudBees SDK version: 1.5.0
# CloudBees Driver version: 1.3.6
Name                GroupId                         Version

ant-plugin          org.cloudbees.sdk.plugins       1.3.0
app-plugin          org.cloudbees.sdk.plugins       1.5.2
config-plugin       org.cloudbees.sdk.plugins       1.3.2
db-plugin           org.cloudbees.sdk.plugins       1.3.2
service-plugin      com.cloudbees.sdk.plugins       1.2.2
```

Plugins allow SDK to be extended with higher-level features or service-specific commands. This book is not a technical guide to writing plugins, so we won't go further into the details, just demonstrate how extensibility provides valuable features.

Blue-green deployment

When you redeploy your application, the router switches traffic to the new application, as it's ready to accept HTTP requests. This zero-downtime deployment is useful but may not fulfill all use cases. Even with a conscientious development and test process, you may want to manually validate new instances of health and behavior and then switch traffic. You may also want to switch traffic only at a specific time or keep previous version up and running as a backup in case some unexpected issue occurs. This can also be useful for applications that take time to set up, so if they can't actually serve the users' requests even when the servlet container is up-and-running, the HTTP traffic is switched.

Blue-green deployment, as documented by Martin Fowler (`http://martinfowler.com/bliki/BlueGreenDeployment.html`), suggests that we keep versions N and $N + 1$ for an application running concurrently and manage the version upgrade from the frontend reverse proxy. With this setup, the new version of the application can be tested and validated, after which the administrator can switch traffic and roll back if needed.

Such a hot reverse-proxy reconfiguration can be implemented on CloudBees using the `sdk app:router:update` command, but requires some logic to determine the blue-green application and provide the appropriate parameters.

CloudBees engineer Fabian Donze created an SDK plugin to support this deployment scenario, and contributed it as `bg-plugin` (`https://github.com/CloudBees-community/bees-cli-bg-plugin`).

With this plugin, setting up a blue-green deployment process can be fully automated from a Jenkins build. We first need to set up SDK and `bg-plugin`:

```
bees plugin:install com.cloudbees.sdk.plugins:bg-plugin
```

Then we run the actual application deployment but using the `app:bg:deploy` command:

```
# DEPLOY
bees app:bg:deploy -n packt target/web-webapp.war
```

This command is comparable to `app:deploy`, by uses the `-n` option to select a blue-green application group.

The DNS is configured for `packt.loof.fr` that is, my own personal domain) to resolve the HTTP requests, and `packt-offline.loof.fr` to resolve the inactive application. We can use this to wait for the new app to be up and running (as initialization may be a long process) and then switch the HTTP traffic:

```
# WARM NEW SERVERS
echo "Preparing new servers for router switch over..."
for i in {1..50}
do
    curl -s "http://packt-offline.loof.fr/" > /dev/null
    sleep 5
done


# SWITCH ROUTER
echo "Switching router over to new servers..."
bees app:bg:switch -n packt -f


# SHUTDOWN OLD SERVERS
echo "Shutting down old servers..."
bees app:bg:stop -n packt -f
```

In this script, we ran some simple SDK commands but actually implemented an advanced deployment scenario, thanks to the SDK plugin that manages most of the complexity.

Let's stop talking about the command line. This one gives you advanced options, but for daily application development you will probably use a graphical IDE and expect CloudBees tooling to be available here as well.

IDE integration

We'll now have a look at the two most common IDEs in Java and how they are integrated with CloudBees.

Eclipse plugin

Eclipse is the most used IDE for Java development, with a large plugin ecosystem to adapt to various use cases. CloudBees has developed its own plugin, so you don't need to leave the comfortable graphical environment in order to integrate with the services.

Installation

The CloudBees plugin is available in Eclipse Marketplace. You can search for `cloudbees` or just open `https://marketplace.eclipse.org/content/cloudbees-toolkit-eclipse` and drag the **install** link into your Eclipse workspace. This will automatically open the installer component selection, which looks like this:

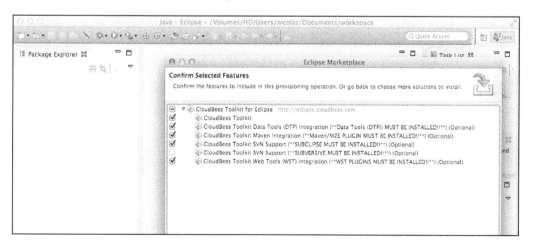

The CloudBees plugin has multiple optional components to integrate with various Eclipse technologies:

- **Data Tools Integration :** This adds support to CloudBees-hosted MySQL from Eclipse DTP, so you can manage the database schema and data from the IDE

- **Maven integration :** This extends M2Eclipse with CloudBees-specific goals

- **Subversion Support :** This is split into two optional components, as Eclipse has two of them, so you have to choose one (**sic**)

- **Web Tools Integration :** This adds support to CloudBees apps in WTP, so you can deploy the application in one click and check the health from the IDE

 The optional component prerequisites must be installed prior to running this installation wizard.

After installation and the usual Eclipse restart, the Eclipse preference lets you log in to CloudBees using your account credentials. Please note, if you created an account using Google or GitHub integration, you have to define a password on GrandCentral and validate your account as shown in the following screenshot:

The CloudBees view

The Eclipse plugin CloudBees view offers a dashboard of your CloudBees services. This dashboard has the following components:

- **Builds** lets you monitor your DEV@cloud Jenkins instance. **Local Builds** can also be used to monitor a classic Jenkins instance running on premises.

- **Applications** shows you deployed applications on RUN@cloud with status, and right-clicking on it lets you run the base commands and access logs.

- **DataBases** shows you the hosted database and an option to connect to it using Eclipse DTP.

- **Repositories** shows you Git and the subversion repositories on the CloudBees forge, with the option to check out. Please note, if you run behind a corporate proxy, you might have to select **http** as protocol to access the Git repositories in the Eclipse CloudBees configuration.

Let's select the **packt** repository in the forge section and check out. The Eclipse Git wizard assists us to select the check out location and branch and then import the project option.

ClickStart integration

The CloudBees Eclipse plugin also provides integration for ClickStart, so you can benefit from the quick experience of setting up a project without leaving the editor. Eclipse UI is not as radical as the web ClickStart wizard, but has a comparable result, as you can see in the following screenshot:

The CloudBees plugin will then run ClickStart behind the scenes, clone the Git repository locally, and import project into the workspace. Wait for the famous Eclipse progress bar pop up to show the process to be completed. Then you're ready to code.

You can see a demonstration of using the CloudBees Eclipse plugin thanks to the video by Mark: http://www.youtube.com/watch?v=ZWLqdQKpmbA

IntelliJ Idea support

JetBrains Intellij Idea is the second most used Java IDE, with a large community of fans to claim its evident superiority compared to Eclipse (I'm one of them).

Idea provides within default installation a CloudBees-dedicated plugin (developed by JetBrains) to support deployment to PaaS. CloudBees is available as a target application server from the IDE, and lets you configure the account and application as well as the action to perform after deployment. We typically open the browser in the JavaScript debug mode to give the deployed application a try and diagnose the possible issues:

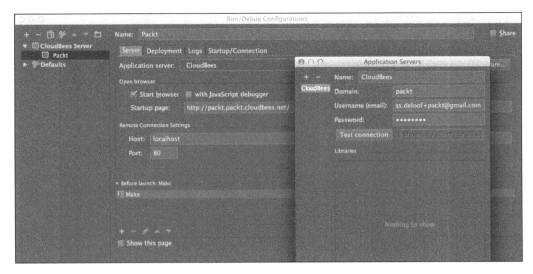

For sure the JetBrain CloudBees plugin has far less features compared to Eclipse one, but with the continuous deployment setup by ClickStart, you don't really need more than a `git push` command.

Read more about this plugin in the JetBrains official documentation at `http://confluence.jetbrains.com/display/IntelliJIDEA/CloudBees`.

GitHub integration

GitHub is the de facto reference for open source Git hosting and a highly valuable service for collaborative development. CloudBees developed a dedicated DEV@cloud simplified clone for GitHub users called **BuildHive**.

BuildHive is a hosted **Continuous Integration** (**CI**) service dedicated to GitHub. You just need to log in within BuildHive from your GitHub account and select repositories you want CI to be enabled on. BuildHive will detect the project type, set up a job for you, and configure commit hooks to trigger a build as you push changes in the repository as shown in the following screenshot:

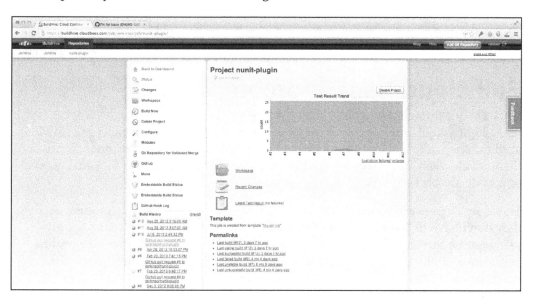

As a bonus feature, BuildHive will also monitor pull requests and provide the build status to the pull-request UI as shown in the following screenshot, so you don't need to spend much time reviewing when a pull request fails to validate:

Full cloud-based toolbox

Software development evolves quickly, and we see more and more developers using lightweight languages and frameworks, developing pure JavaScript/HTML5 applications without the requirement for a heavy-load desktop computer. Some of them would even like to develop using a tablet or ChromeBook, as they just need to edit some simple script files.

Those developers are fans of GitHub, CloudBees, and comparable providers as they don't have to install anything on the local computer; they can manage only using online services. There are interesting efforts to provide a comparable online experience for the IDE. GitHub even provides an online editor, which is useful when you only need to edit a file, but it quickly hits limitations.

CodeEnvy mimics Eclipse IDE's look and feel for Java developers to comfortably migrate to the Cloud-based service. After adding a private SSH key to the account, you can check out the project from the CloudBees Git repository. After few seconds, the online IDE displays the project structure and lets you edit code, prepare a commit, and then push for the change to CloudBees as shown in the following screenshot:

Summary

This chapter demonstrated the use of SDK and IDE integration as daily tools to provide a convenient experience as a CloudBees application developer. SDK wasn't covered in detail, as this would require a whole book by itself, but you'll discover the available features by giving it a try yourself and adapting to your own development process.

8

Using ClickStack to Extend the Platform

CloudBees claims to be *The Java PaaS company,* focusing on creating a full featured as a service platform for Java developers. Even with this in mind, the platform is flexible enough to cover a larger set of runtimes and frameworks.

DEV@cloud Jenkins is the de facto continuous integration server for Java developers, but it is being adopted by other ecosystems as well. With a plugin-based architecture, it can be adapted to build in PHP, Ruby, Python, or any other language.

RUN@cloud gets inspired by this design and evolves to offer a modular architecture, letting developers provide customization on a base system so that they can extend the platform to cover alternate runtimes.

By looking at the ClickStart official wizard, you can see the extent to which this principle was successful. CloudBees can host the Play Framework, Grails, a large set of Java EE/Servlet containers, and also non-JVM based runtimes such as Node.js, PHP, Go, Dart, and Erlang.

The following screenshot demonstrates the various stack available on CloudBees, both JVM and non JVM-based stacks:

The RUN@cloud architecture

RUN@cloud uses a layered and extensible architecture. A low-level, infrastructure-aware layer is written in Erlang, which manages server allocation and resource sharing. It's a general purpose layer, which is not tied to a specific runtime. ClickStack runs on top of it and provides runtime specialization. A typical ClickStack will handle the preparation of a Java EE application server, but it could set up a non-JVM-based runtime as well. An application is installed on this runtime. Metadata provides all the required information for each layer to provide adequate resources, and exposes them to the upper layer.

The lower level of the architecture includes GenApp, a low-level process orchestrator written in Erlang. It receives deployment API application commands with metadata on the application to be deployed. Read more about it at `http://genapp-docs.cloudbees.com/`.

ClickStack executes on top of GenApp. ClickStack is responsible for setting up the runtime environment, installing the application, and providing the Bootstrap script.

The application is packaged as a ZIP or WAR archive and runs on a ClickStack-provisioned runtime. The following diagram represents the RUN@cloud architecture:

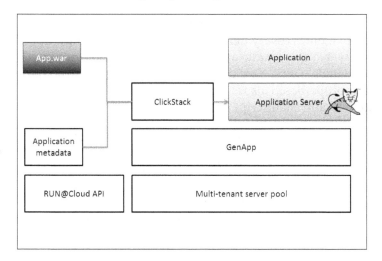

ClickStack from the point of view of GenApp is very simple. Being packaged as a ZIP archive available on a public URL, ClickStack must expose a `setup` executable file (in most cases, a shell script) that GenApp will call during runtime initialization. As a part of initialization, ClickStack is responsible for creating a `control/Start` executable script that GenApp will execute to run the application.

GenApp defines few other optional control scripts to produce application states (displayed in the RUN@cloud web console), invoke administrative commands, or gracefully shut down the stack.

With such a simple contact, you can understand the flexibility of the platform. Node.js ClickStack (`https://github.com/CloudBees-community/nodejs-clickstack`) just has to download the adequate runtime and expand the archive, unzip the application package, and then create a `control/start` shell script to execute the `main.js` node.

Most ClickStacks share a common pattern as follows:

1. Create the application skeleton including applications, controls, libraries, and directories.

2. Install the runtime after being downloaded from a public URL, usually from Amazon S3 to avoid deployment delays.

3. Create a configuration file for the installed runtime based on the application's metadata.

4. Install the deployed application.

5. Create control scripts.

A complex ClickStack such as JBoss has to download the JBoss distribution archive, expand and remove unnecessary default applications, expand the application's WAR archive as a sole webapp, generate a `standalone.xml` configuration file based on the application metadata, and then provide the `control/start` script with preset adequate system properties. This requires significant code and usually can't be addressed within a pure shell script.

The following schema summarizes the ClickStack architecture and its responsibilities. The GenApp agent sets up server resources, creates a dedicated application folder, and copyies both the deployed application ZIP file and the configured ClickStack. It then executes the `setup` script and lets the ClickStack handle runtime preparation. This agent has to manage the possible complexity of this task on its own. GenApp then executes the `control/start` script and monitors the associated process.

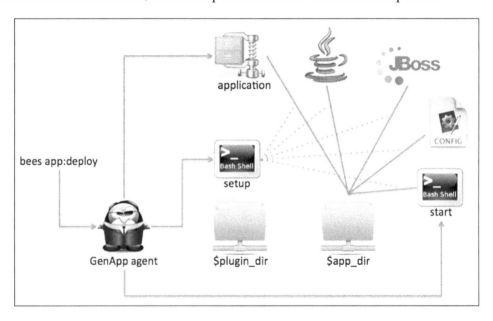

Metadata

The deployed applications are configured with the CloudBees resources such as Database, SendGrid mail service, and application parameters. ClickStack has to manage this by generating the adequate runtime configuration and the `control/start` script so that the application has the expected resources included.

By invoking GenApp to set up an application during deployment, the CloudBees RUN@cloud service provides the application's metadata as a JSON file. The `metadata.json` file contains all the account information, configured resources, and application parameters.

Here is an excerpt for such a metadata file:

```
{
  "sendgrid": {
    "__resource_type__": "email",
    "SENDGRID_SMTP_HOST": "smtp.sendgrid.net",
    "__resource_name__": "mail\/SendGrid",
    "SENDGRID_USERNAME": "cloudbees_packt",
    "SENDGRID_PASSWORD": "abcdef1234"
  },
  "saucelabs": {
    "id": "packt",
    "__resource_type__": "saucelabs",
    "minutes": "200",
    "__resource_name__": "saucelabs",
    "access_key": "c7b7d7e7-1234-abcd-5678-3c4c5c6c7c8c"
  },
  "cloudant": {
    "server_address": https:\/\/packt.cloudbees.cloudant.com",
    "__resource_type__": "cloudant",
    "username": "nicolas.cloudbees",
    "__resource_name__": "cloudant",
    "password": "abcdef1234567890abcdef1234567890"
  },
  ...
```

The metadata file displays access URLs, credentials, and other subscription parameters for all the CloudBees services so that your application can retrieve them at runtime or simply get ClickStack to display them in a convenient way.

The directory structure

The application deployed on RUN@cloud gets a dedicated directory, which is exposed as a `$app_dir` environment variable. GenApp is responsible for the isolation of the application and creates the application. It also creates a `.genapp` (`$genapp_dir`) subfolder to store the control scripts, metadata, and logs.

The deployed application archive (WAR, EAR, or ZIP, depending on ClickStack) is copied into `$pkg_dir`.

Plugins are copied into a $plugin_dir folder to prepare the setup execution. As the setup is run, the plugin's setup output is logged under $log_dir (.genapp/log) for diagnostic purposes.

GenApp allocates a port for the deployed application and configures a router to route the HTTP traffic to this port for the incoming request to match the application hostname. The selected port is displayed as an $app_port environment variable. It also displays the application identifier $app_id and the $app_user Unix user to run the application.

As parsing JSON from a Bash script isn't trivial, GenApp also displays the metadata as environment variables. It uses a *keyword style* algorithm so that the nested elements of JSON are prefixed by the parent with an underscore separator. So, the following will be displayed as a logging_file environment variable:

```
"logging": {
  "file": "server.log"
}
```

Plugins

The previous examples explained how ClickStack sets up the runtime for an application, but you can have more than one active ClickStack for an application. You can't mix anything together, but some ClickStacks are just plugins and don't try to change the control/start script. They only provide some additional configuration files and libraries. This allows, for example, the NewRelic CloudBees partner to plug into a Java application, providing a JVM agent and container configuration.

From the point of view of GenApp, all ClickStacks are plugins as long as running the setup script for each of them produces the expected control/start script. It's all up to the ClickStacks to operate together nicely. In some cases, this script is required to display some hooks for other ClickStacks in order to contribute additional features.

ClickStack by sample

Based on the existing samples in the CloudBees-community GitHub organization, you can quickly create your own ClickStack. Let's introduce you to ClickStack development.

A simple ClickStack plugin

We will create a very basic ClickStack plugin as an introductory tutorial. This one doesn't need to set up runtime; it is just a plugin, but gives you the base for later development.

The RUN@cloud servers provide a minimalistic, stable Linux environment. To enforce tenant isolation, both your application and ClickStack run without root permissions. Java developers use ClickStack to embed a dozen utility libraries into WAR, but sometimes you need to use native code. For example, you may need to process video streams using the `ffmpeg` library.

You can retrieve this sample stack from `https://github.com/ndeloof/ffmpeg-clickstack`. This ClickStack has only one significant file. The first file is the `setup` script that will be used as it is by GenApp. This is a trivial shell script:

```
echo "Installing ffmpeg"
cp $plugin_dir/ffmpeg $app_dir
```

You might notice the use of an environment variable for the current plugin directory when the `setup` script is executed which targets the application directory.

Other files to consider are the `Makefile` and `plugin.mk` files used to package and deploy the ClickStack. The setup based on `MakeFile` is not a requirement; use your preferred build tool to pack your ClickStacks as long as it fulfills the GenApp expectations. `Makefile` and `plugin.mk` are just a convenient way used by CloudBees engineering on most ClickStacks to avoid repetition.

If you look at `Makefile`, you'll notice that the actual preparation is as follows:

```
ffmpeg_url=http://ffmpeg.gusari.org/static/64bit/ffmpeg.
static.64bit.2013-08-25.tar.gz
lib/ffmpeg:
  mkdir -p lib
  curl -fLo lib/ffmpeg.tar.gz "$(ffmpeg_url)"
  (cd lib; tar -xzf ffmpeg.tar.gz)
```

Indeed, this ClickStack role is to provide the `ffmpeg` binaries with a runtime environment, but it has to work around two major constraints:

- To avoid application deployment delays, plugin should embed all the required resources. Downloading from an external URL will slow down the GenApp setup.

- As ClickStack and the application don't grant root permissions, you need to provide statically compiled binaries. Most Linux software is only distributed as system packages, so you may have to compile them from the sources.

After being packaged as a ZIP file, your ClickStack has to be uploaded to a public URL for GenApp to retrieve it. For your convenience, you can use `https://clickstack-repository.cloudbees.com/` to upload your ClickStack, and test it using the following code:

```
bees app:deploy -a appid -t yourstack -RPLUGIN.SRC.yourstack=url
```

Community and contributions

Some ClickStacks are classified as curated. These stacks offer all the CloudBees' features (resource introduction, auto-scaling, private mode, and so on) and are fully supported. This includes Tomcat 6, JBoss 7, and Java standalone ClickStacks.

Other ClickStacks are managed by CloudBees, which means that engineering actively improves them and supports customers, but some CloudBees' features may not be implemented. This includes Play2, Node.js, or Tomcat 7 ClickStacks.

The community supports the remaining ClickStacks. If you look at committers on the CloudBees-community GitHub repository, where all the ClickStacks are hosted, you'll notice that CloudBees engineering has created most of them, providing samples for contributors. Some are pure community contributions, such as Dart.

All ClickStacks are open source, so you can fork one to improve or adapt to the custom needs and maybe contribute back, so it can benefit other users. You can join `cloudbees-dev@googlegroups.com` to discuss directly with engineers on implementation details or ask for assistance on deployment issues.

Advanced ClickStack

Sharing the code

As I have described the JBoss ClickStack setup as a complex setup process, you may have noticed that I omitted a major step: I didn't talk about installing JVM to run Tomcat.

CloudBees has a Java ClickStack for general purpose Java applications used to deploy non Servlet-based applications. But the JBoss ClickStack (`https://github.com/CloudBees-community/java-clickstack`) can't be used in combination with Java ClickStack (two-active GenApp plugins) as both of them will try to create the `control/start` script.

As a workaround, JBoss directly embeds the Java ClickStack plugin. Similar to most of the ClickStacks, this one's `setup` script only invokes the lower-level functions, and this lets JBoss ClickStack to re-use them for setting up both the Java runtime and JBoss container.

Sharing code within ClickStack is not homogeneous and depends on the developer's habits. Tomcat 7 uses Git submodules to include Java ClickStack and invoke its setup functions. Some include a `git` clone command in `Makefile`. Use your preferred approach.

Complex setup

Some ClickStacks have to support a complex setup process. Most Java EE application container ClickStacks have to tweak the container to add some additional libraries and generate configuration files. This is sometimes difficult to address within a shell script, so they rely on invoking the Java setup code to parse `metadata.json` and manipulate the container's XML configuration files.

Tomcat 8 ClickStack (`https://github.com/CloudBees-community/tomcat8-clickstack`) went deep into this approach. Tomcat 8 ClickStack is a pure Java project built with Gradle. The `Setup.java` file provides a main method to be invoked by GenApp that fully handles the preparation of the application runtime. Thanks to the Java object-oriented language and helper libraries that made it easy to parse `metadata.json`, create a container skeleton, and tweak the `context.xml` configuration file.

```java
public static void main(String[] args) throws Exception {
//...
  Path metadataPath = genappDir.resolve("metadata.json");
  Metadata metadata = Metadata.Builder.fromFile(metadataPath);
  Setup setup = new Setup(appDir, clickstackDir, packageDir);
  setup.installSkeleton();
  Path catalinaBase = setup.installCatalinaBase();
  setup.installCatalinaHome();
  setup.installCloudBeesJavaAgent();
  setup.installJmxTransAgent();
  setup.writeJavaOpts(metadata);
  setup.writeConfig(metadata, appPort);
  setup.installControlScripts();
  setup.installTomcatJavaOpts();
  ContextXmlBuilder contextXmlBuilder = new
    ContextXmlBuilder(metadata);
  contextXmlBuilder.
    buildTomcatConfigurationFiles(catalinaBase);
```

Gradle is used to build this ClickStack as it allows a fine control on the dependencies to add the required libraries in to the container depending on the bound resources. For example, if you bind a `PostgreSQL` database to a Tomcat 8 application, ClickStack will create a `DataSource` object, and will add the required JDBC driver to the container's common classes.

Using the Java ecosystem, build tools and helper libraries demonstrate a significant improvement in ClickStack's flexibility to address more complex runtime constraints. Depending on your goal of writing a ClickStack, for runtime customization needs and you favorite development language, you can choose to either use a simple shell script or a higher-level development language.

Testing

Writing a trivial `ffmpeg` ClickStack is easy, and testing it directly on RUN@cloud with a demo application is fine. For more complex stacks, you'll need some way to test and diagnose them.

The local GenApp installation

GenApp is an open source framework and is well documented at `http://genapp-docs.cloudbees.com/`. You can install a local GenApp to test your ClickStack plugins. As RUN@cloud's target environment is Arch Linux, it won't make much sense to give it a try if you don't use a Linux or an OS X system. Running on Windows using Cygwin may work, but it is not the best option.

Follow the *Quick Start* guide (`http://genapp-docs.cloudbees.com/quickstart.html`) to get an overview of the use of GenApp and ensure that everything is working fine in your environment.

GenApp uses Erlang and Python; so, as a prerequisite, associated runtime must be installed. You don't have to worry as you don't need to write much Erlang code to test a ClickStack. Deploying an application on a local GenApp is all about typing a basic command in the Erlang interactive shell as follows:

```
> genapp:deploy("HOME_DIR/genapp/sample-app")
```

If everything is fine, you'll get an application prepared under `~/genapp/apps/APP_ID/` and can manually run the `control/start` script.

Automated tests

Tomcat 8 ClickStack follows a full-Java approach; it uses Gradle as a build tool and fully implements the setup within Java code. This allows writing unit tests, especially checking the metadata of container-specific configuration files so that you don't need to actually deploy the ClickStack to discover a regression—not a promise that you will *never* discover a regression, but you will avoid some of them.

Another option is to rely on integration tests; configuring a Jenkins job to build the ClickStack, deploying a RUN@cloud sample application to use it, and running some smoke tests to ensure that the application behaves as expected with the adequate runtime that is set.

Summary

This chapter demonstrated the flexibility of the CloudBees platform to support various runtimes and adapt to the customer's needs. ClickStack lets you take control of the lower-level infrastructure details, configuring your runtime and middleware. Once this is done for all the applications, a ClickStack can be improved by adding support for various use cases and integrating it with the CloudBees advanced services and options.

This chapter concludes our exploration of the CloudBees platform. ClickStack, ClickStart, and ecosystem partners offer a complimentary set of tools for you to create your own toolbox. This is how CloudBees considers the PaaS paradigm shift. You don't have to manage infrastructure and you also don't have to manage middleware. You can now focus on application logic and service integration without loosing the option to fine-tune your runtime when required. This flexibility is the key to modern application development.

Index

G

genapp 65
GitHub
  integrating 79, 80
Google App Engine
  URL 14
Google Mail 8

H

HttpSession servlet
  using 60
httpVersion parameter 70

I

IaaS
  about 7
  benefit 7
  drawback 8
IDE
  integrating 75-79
IDE integration
  Eclipse plugin 75-78
  IntelliJ Idea 78, 79
Infrastructure as a Service. *See* IaaS
integrated partners services
  about 27
  NewRelic service 30
  PaperTrail service 30
  SendGrid service 30
  subscription 28

J

javax.jdbc.DataSource feature 72
Jenkins
  about 45
  automation 46
  CI 45
  extensibility 46
  scalability 46
Jenkins customization 48, 49
Jenkins job
  chaining 52, 53
JetBrains Intellij Idea
  about 78

features 79
URL 79
jvmFileEncoding parameter 70
jvmPermSize parameter 70
jvmTimeZone parameter 70

L

local GenApp
  installing, to test ClickStack plugins 92
logging_file variable 88

M

m1.micro instance 24
Maven archetype 22
monitoring 64

O

on-demand slaves 50

P

PaaS
  about 9
  versus, self-managed infrastructure 23, 24
persistent filesystem 62
platform 10
Platform as a Service. *See* PaaS
private Cloud
  versus, public Cloud 11
project
  building 36, 37
promotion plugin 53
Promotion process window 54
public Cloud
  versus, private Cloud 11, 12
PuTTY
  used, for SSH key generating 18, 19

R

RBAC 26
resource
  binding 72
  managing 72

Thank you for buying
Cloud Development and Deployment with CloudBees

About Packt Publishing

Packt, pronounced 'packed', published its first book "*Mastering phpMyAdmin for Effective MySQL Management*" in April 2004 and subsequently continued to specialize in publishing highly focused books on specific technologies and solutions.

Our books and publications share the experiences of your fellow IT professionals in adapting and customizing today's systems, applications, and frameworks. Our solution based books give you the knowledge and power to customize the software and technologies you're using to get the job done. Packt books are more specific and less general than the IT books you have seen in the past. Our unique business model allows us to bring you more focused information, giving you more of what you need to know, and less of what you don't.

Packt is a modern, yet unique publishing company, which focuses on producing quality, cutting-edge books for communities of developers, administrators, and newbies alike. For more information, please visit our website: www.packtpub.com.

About Packt Open Source

In 2010, Packt launched two new brands, Packt Open Source and Packt Enterprise, in order to continue its focus on specialization. This book is part of the Packt Open Source brand, home to books published on software built around Open Source licences, and offering information to anybody from advanced developers to budding web designers. The Open Source brand also runs Packt's Open Source Royalty Scheme, by which Packt gives a royalty to each Open Source project about whose software a book is sold.

Writing for Packt

We welcome all inquiries from people who are interested in authoring. Book proposals should be sent to author@packtpub.com. If your book idea is still at an early stage and you would like to discuss it first before writing a formal book proposal, contact us; one of our commissioning editors will get in touch with you.

We're not just looking for published authors; if you have strong technical skills but no writing experience, our experienced editors can help you develop a writing career, or simply get some additional reward for your expertise.

Learning Play! Framework 2

ISBN: 978-1-78216-012-0   Paperback: 290 pages

Start developing awesome web applications with this friendly, practical guide to the Play! Framework

1. While driving in Java, tasks are also presented in Scala – a great way to be introduced to this amazing language

2. Create a fully-fledged, collaborative web application – starting from ground zero; all layers are presented in a pragmatic way

3. Gain the advantages associated with developing a fully integrated web framework

Instant Play Framework Starter

ISBN: 978-1-78216-290-2   Paperback: 70 pages

Build your web applications from the ground up with the Play Framework for Java and Scala

1. Learn something new in an Instant! A short, fast, focused guide delivering immediate results

2. Get started with Play 2.1

3. Build your own web application with Java and Scala

4. Handle user input with forms and access data with Ebean, Anorm, and Slick

Please check **www.PacktPub.com** for information on our titles

Ext JS 4 Web Application Development Cookbook

ISBN: 978-1-84951-686-0   Paperback: 488 pages

Over 110 easy-to-follow receipes backed up with real-life examples, walking you through basic Ext JS features to advanced application design using Sencha's Ext JS

1. Learn how to build Rich Internet Applications with the latest version of the Ext JS framework in a cookbook style

2. From creating forms to theming your interface, you will learn the building blocks for developing the perfect web application

3. Easy to follow recipes step through practical and detailed examples which are all fully backed up with code, illustrations, and tips

Akka Essentials

ISBN: 978-1-84951-828-4   Paperback: 334 pages

A practical, step-by-step guide to learn and build Akka's actor-based, distributed, concurrent, and scalable Java applications

1. Build large, distributed, concurrent, and scalable applications using the Akka's Actor model

2. Simple and clear analogy to Java/JEE application development world to explain the concepts

3. Each chapter will teach you a concept by explaining it with clear and lucid examples- each chapter can be read independently

Please check **www.PacktPub.com** for information on our titles